The Self-Builder's Guide To The Construction Phase

Vince Holden

Published by Holden Management.

Cover Design by Team Boult

ISBN 13: 978-0-9934064-2-3 Paperback
978-0-9934064-3-0 ebook

For Little Lil and Bella Brush

Vince Holden

About this Book

My previous book, The Self-Builders Guide to Project Management, was created following my many years as a building main contractor, working mainly on new builds, but also on sizeable refurbs and conversions, which led me to follow the path of a project manager.

I played the role of builder quite literally for decades, working with numerous architects, engineers, developers, private clients, Building Control, warranty surveyors, conservation officers, tradesman, builders, merchants ... the list is endless. But for almost as many years, I felt that all these ingredients lacked cohesion, relying upon the proficiency of the builder; his relationship with the client, architect, and other professionals; his want to try to bridge the gaps; a large portion of luck; and the dependence on the making-it-up-as-you-go-along mantra. I filled those gaps – even though not really my role – and to the best of my knowledge, I filled them adequately.

I realised quite simply that there is so much information required between the designer(s), client, and builder and too many holes in the collation of this information.

However, as the scale of work increases from say extensions and modernisations, up through large refurbs and new builds, so does the importance for someone to glue it all together. This required management role escalates also with the inclusion of recent energy performance requirements, the coming (and going) of the Code for Sustainable Homes, ever-changing building regulations and planning policies, and most importantly, the thirst of Mr & Mrs Self Build (SB) to build their own dream home comprising renewable technologies and low running costs.

So, this is where the project manager and this book come in. I decided that there was a necessity for some place that Mr and Mrs SB, wanting to manage their own project, could go to find lots of information and advice, and learn about the many potential obstacles that could arise in the process, so that they could tackle their build process and supervision but retain their own hair and sanity.

The previous book explored and explained many of the works involved in navigating the pre-construction phase, and therefore, aimed to get you ready to tackle the construction phase.

That's where this book takes over!

My inspiration comes from not only my technical knowledge learned over many years, but also from the practical construction experience gleaned from four decades or so at the cutting edge of (cue Chariots of Fir music) site works and the people involved. To work with probably some of the strangest people to walk this earth has been nothing short of a privilege, which has given me the insight to share with you the mentality and motives of your average (or less) building worker.

My intention is to explain the method – not so much of the mechanics of the trade itself but more the people involved – that will help you understand the best way to plan and initiate your build. It is very important that you tune into the mentality of the 'builder worker', and for those of you not experienced in such matters, it will probably help if you watch some children's telly for a while to acclimatise your mind.

We will explore the many aspects of managing the construction process. I will teach you how to physically lay bricks or mix concrete, but I believe that I have addressed most elements to help you understand what is achievable and how to ensure that works are completed correctly.

Hopefully with the aid of this book, the build process stands a decent chance of arriving at its destination without crashing. The construction phase of building or refurbishing your home is a huge task, with the amount of knowledge and awareness required for the process very often misunderstood and hugely underestimated. Therefore, using the ensuing information and access to my knowledge base*, you can be in control and avoid nasty surprises, ensuring that you reach the end of your build with a project you are proud of and all your nerves intact.

*By buying this book, you receive exclusive rights to contact me for free expert advice on any of the subjects covered – see end of the book for details.
∏

Vince Holden

CONTENTS

Vince Holden

Part 1

You don't know what you don't know

Vince Holden

1

The Self-builder and the Project Manager

For the benefit of those of you who have not read *The Self-Builders Guide to Project Management*, I will briefly outline what I mean by a self-builder.

The self-build concept has existed in many forms for just about as long as construction works themselves.

However, over the past 10 years or so, Mr and Mrs SB have wanted to, and been practicably able to, become completely involved in the entire process. They no longer need to buy a new house designed by others, built to a standard that could later prove questionable. They can now choose exactly what items are important, be it sustainability and renewable technology or the level of IT goodies. So with the correct level of advice and input, the world is your oyster as the self-builder.

To contemplate a major refurb or build an entire house from scratch takes commitment, courage, and a robust mind-set. I am not referring to your ability to lay a brick or hang a door. This book is dedicated to the managerial skills required to organise the works, deal with the people, and understand the importance of the correct processes. You neither need computer processor thinking power, nor master construction as an exact science; you (relatively) simply need a strong working understanding of the procedures, choices, and knowledge requirements of the project. There are tricks and there are banana skins, but with the right information and guidance, you can develop the required skills to manage these numerous elements.

This book will give even the most nervous first-timer correct and useful information to build their home.

There are fundamentally two different ways forward with the self-build process and with it, two requirements to manage this process.

The simple way forward is to obtain your project, place all your preamble ducks in a row, then employ a builder as a main contractor to effectively take over from there. The amount of involvement from you towards the preambles is of course your choice, and some would prefer to simply employ an architectural practice to handle just about everything – from planning to handing over the keys at the end. But of course, this is not self-building, and without doubt, it comes at a cost.

To an extent, the builder would assist with some elements of the pre-construction works for you, and therefore, handle the project management. Whilst technically this is still self-build, you are giving up control to the builder, and with it, the satisfaction of knowing that you created the end product. Also, by deciding to use a building contractor, you are dramatically reducing your own input and with it, the knowledge and control, both in terms of cost and specification.

The second and most exciting way is to obtain the project, have a significant input in the design and execution of the pre-construction requirements, and then manage the whole construction phase yourself with sub-contractors, up to the end. This to me is the most invigorating way, but it is clearly not for the faint-hearted. This way forward is where high competence in project management is absolutely essential, and you really do need to know your onions. You do not want to fire fight your way through the project, but carefully plan and manage each element with confidence and strength. I have over forty years of experience; you probably don't, otherwise you would not be reading this book. But it does not take all that time to understand, plan and manage your build if you have the right tools at hand.

With the knowledge gleaned from this book, an investment of time, and the correct attitude, you will be able to see your project take shape right before your eyes, knowing that all bases are covered and you have controlled as much as possible.

In the previous book, I covered the preambles and provided you with a valuable understanding of the workings of self-building. This book will put this knowledge to good use and give you the confidence to take the job forward into the construction phase.

What is a construction project manager? Can you manage a construction project yourself, or do you need to outsource it?

By buying this book, you are indicating that having read the first book, you still feel that the role is for you. However, this is a task easily underestimated, requiring at least a basic understanding of construction methods, but equally important is the sense to realise that the majority of the aspects of self-building involve professionals with many years of experience.

The clever self-builders will know which professionals are needed and which are not.

The Project Manager

Project management is the application of processes, methods, knowledge, skills, and experience to achieve the project objectives. A project is a unique, transient endeavour, undertaken to achieve planned objectives, which could be defined in terms of outputs, outcomes, or benefits.

Or to put it simply, project management involves making sure that the right person is in the right place doing the right job with the right materials for the right cost at the right time.

The project manager will need to work with anyone involved in the build. This will include building control officers, conservation officers, and any other environmental representatives. They will also need to interact constantly with the design team to deal with any design issues or alterations that may occur during construction.

The management of a construction project needs a particular set of skills. The project manager will need to carry out their duties appropriately and with enthusiasm. They must be able to motivate, and yet maintain discipline. They need a variety of technical skills to be able to solve any problems when they occur and to keep the whole project rolling forward.

Then there is Programme Management, which is essential to the smooth running of any project during the construction period. It can be carried out remotely, as long as there is someone on site who can provide all the required information to the relevant parties. It is only by keeping a wary eye on everything, though, that the build will continue to run smoothly.

Unless you have many years of experience in construction in terms of both the mechanics and the management, there will be elements where you require knowledgeable help. Whether it's knowing how to actually navigate the pre-construction process, or understanding the mechanism of the build and the sub-contractors, you will need that knowledge. You will need to be able to foster a team spirit, where it has to be appreciated by all concerned that they need you as much as you need them.

Now I am not trying to discourage you from taking up this role – this book is aimed at providing you with practical advice; but part of that advice is know your limitations. There may be aspects that you can happily tick off yourself, and there may be some that you cannot. The good manager will delegate certain parts but will at least understand what they are.

Hopefully, by the time you have read this book, you will have filtered what you can do from what is beyond your capabilities.

2

Before You Begin

Before you start your project, think of yourself as the conductor of an orchestra. You are putting together a production with many elements and many moving parts. The more attention you pay to the details in the early stages, the less likely you are to encounter problems, delays, or errors in the finished product. Your musicians are looking to you for direction – never forget that everything depends on timing.

Maestro

The young maestro steps up to the lectern and takes the general arrangement music score from his bag. This is not the original as created by the composer; this is the eventual version fashioned from numerous discussions and research with both the composer and some of the key instrument section leaders. Maestro has a vision of exactly what he wants to create, so with their inputs, he adjusts and re-adjusts until it is perfect.

The maestro's version has many marks and notes on it that only he would understand, but that's OK. The key leaders will have their own versions relevant only to them. Maestro has copies of them in his bag also, to be taken out and addressed at certain stages of the performance. Also in his bag, young maestro has a well-thumbed copy of a book written by a great virtuoso, which sets out the mechanics of creating such a great performance. Young maestro does not need to consult the book – he knows it inside out and has used it time and time again when preparing for the performance, until he feels knowledgeable on all aspects. He just keeps it with him at all times to give him comfort, and of course refer to if needed.

Likewise, he knows in great detail all of the key instrument sections' music scores – he helped create them, as he decided which musicians to use. The process of making these choices in musicians were sometimes arduous, but by the time each decision was made, young maestro felt confident that the right person was in place. He would start with several of each section leader, whittling it down to the perfect option. He would, in most cases, leave it to the elected section leader to choose their preferred principles and rank-and-file but would nevertheless want his own input.

When making the choices, whilst he appreciated that he personally could not necessarily play the instrument in question, he believed that he had a good ear and knew a true sound when he heard it. However, ultimately, he had to believe in his choice and allow the individual musicians the freedom to create their own portion of the overall performance, knitting together with other sections as directed by the maestro.

The performance of course has a budget; so again, choosing the correct musician for the performance level was paramount. Even if Yehudi Menuhin had been alive, not only could the performance not afford him, his capabilities would have been overkill. Tucked away in maestro's bag is the costing for each and every music section, although by this time, he hopes that he has made the correct decisions.

As with every good performance, timing is critical, and this is one of maestro's main inputs.

On the lectern, alongside his general arrangement is his own programme of the performance showing when each section will begin. If left to their own devices, each section, whilst knowing roughly when to play, would quite probably enter at the wrong time, and whilst maestro knows that this can be disguised, it will take all of his skills to get the performance back on track. No, the way forward is to firmly direct each section, making sure that they are there with their own portion of the performance at exactly the right time, using the correct instruments.

The maestro is nervous. This is his first complete performance; however, he feels that he has chosen well with experienced musicians, and has been able to get to know them and their capabilities. Therefore, he feels sure that he is in good hands. He has created a strong team who will work well together and guide him along as well.

So, with the knowledge that he has prepared as well as he possibly can, the young maestro taps his baton on the lectern, raises his hands, takes a deep breath, looks at every one of them in the eye and ...

3

Sub-contractors (Panusinthearsus)

For you to be able to work with construction workers, whatever they call themselves – contractors, sub-contractors, tradesmen, or labour, you would be wise to get up to speed with their mentality.

The majority of men, and sometimes women, in construction work hard and earn their money, and let's face it, that's why they get up and go to work in the morning – to earn money. As much as possible!. However, the moment we start using words like tradesmen, craftsmen, or contractors, be prepared for him (or occasionally her) to have an ego the size of China and pedantic demands to go with it.

The more time I spend project managing, especially with Mr and Mrs SB, the more I realise that one of the biggest fears you good people have when contemplating embarking on the self-build journey is how to deal with 'the immortal subbie'. At best, he (or she) is a know-all, pedantic prima donna who believes that the entire build hinges around their colossal ability – at worst, they may be bitchy, argumentative, demanding, aggressive, and a downright pain in the backside!

This attitude is not trade-specific. Show me a self-employed tradesman, and I will show you the demigod of the construction industry, who will single-handedly want to dictate the programme of the complete works because everything must hinge around his artistry – when he's there of course!

The situation is being made worse by the ever-depleting stock of formally qualified trades, and in my opinion, it is not going to improve any time soon, with so little new blood coming into the industry. Many formally trained and qualified people are reaching a certain age and, therefore, looking towards throttling back. However, unfortunately, they are not being replaced at the same rate as their decline. Whilst there are still several good quality, motivated, and genuine tradesmen out there, the ratio between good and not so good has seen a downward shift over the past 20 years.

It is easy for me to comment. First, I was formally trained, then I became a subbie tradesman, and subsequently, I spent the majority of my life working with and employing construction workers, so I know what to expect and how to deal with them. But there is no doubt in my mind that as the years have passed and the number of good-quality construction tradesmen have diminished, the self-important attitude of these artists has grown in equal proportions, leaving even seasoned old owls like me needing to tread a bit carefully on occasion.

Apparently, we now have to consider hurting their feelings and so use phrases like 'dignity at work!' and 'stress' – jeez, anyone would think we were all working for John Lewis.

Don't get me wrong – not everyone in the industry behaves in this way. Old school industry pros like me who worked their way up through the ranks the hard way tend to have a more seasoned and pragmatic attitude towards a hard day's work, but whatever happened to being able to call someone a *#@*ing $#**% when something was done wrong, without floods of tears, foot stamping, and storming off. I really don't know what the industry is coming to!

Anyway, back to your works and the subject of using subbies.

The job flows according to your capability to communicate with and anticipate the behaviour of the men doing the works, and whilst I am not suggesting that you take a crash course in builder speak (mmm... now there's a thought for a spinoff!), you will certainly benefit from the ability to discuss your work with confidence and explain your wants with clarity. You would also benefit from being able to demonstrate your ability and standing up for what you want (or not), which is something often exploited by your know-all tradesman, who can often lose sight of who works for whom and who is paying his bill.

Assuming that as per the chapter *Contractor Selection* in Book 1, you have chosen contractors wisely, taking all points in the chapter into consideration, you should be getting ready to be working with a good team of blokes who are on your side and want to simply turn up, get the job done, and get paid. They will still need looking after, though.

Don't be put off by my, dare I say, cynical thoughts above. These people are after all still human (well most of them!) and will respond to courtesy and authoritative discussion without making you become arrogant or frustrated if sometimes all you get is head scratching or grunts in return.

I had a female client a few years ago who insisted on turning up every Friday morning with a box of cream cakes and a tray of teas for whoever was working there that day. At first I tried to discourage it, but soon realised that it went a long way with the blokes. Was it my imagination or was the site always busier on a Friday?

Don't be surprised either, if you hear the occasional profanity (as if!) – the construction workers' language is a cross between broken English and primates (actually with alarming similarities in appearance) and will sometimes offend sensitive ears. If you are likely to be upset by such philosophical semantics, perhaps you would be best placed to buy ear defenders, because believe me, a building site without colourful language simply does not exist. Whatever your disposition, you will need to be prepared to enter into the construction site banter, which simply makes the day go by and the world go round.

I have many years of fond memories during my time on site with the people and the banter. It's in my blood and I miss it, so my advice is to embrace this challenging aspect of your build with your arms wide open ... life will never be the same again!

Your job as newly promoted site manager will be to anticipate the timing of the subbie and guarantee that when he is there, he can get on with the job unimpeded, with all of the detail and information at his fingertips. Ensure that if you are supplying certain materials, they are on-site not too early, not too late, and that they are in the right place. If he is expecting you to have made decisions – large or small (it's the small ones that catch you out) – then make them so that he can push on with the job, making way for the next trade. To keep the subbies and their work flowing is the site manager's main responsibility. Do not underestimate it or its importance when volunteering for the job. We will address this role in the later chapter.

4

Understanding the Drawings and Specifications

So, according to Book 1, you have the detailed drawings, specifications, and schedules, but can you truly read and understand them in a way that complements the objective – to get the works completed efficiently?

The architect or architectural technician will have produced detailed drawings to at least satisfy building control. The drawings will include the following:

- Floor plan: In its basic form, the floor plan will comprise scaled diagrams showing a flat view of the arrangement of rooms from above, one storey at a time. Measurements are usually drawn between walls to indicate room sizes, and are shown in millimetres as opposed to centimetres or metres (for example, 1475 mm as opposed to 147.5 cm or 1.475 m).

- Elevation: This is a view of a building seen from one side – a flat representation of one façade. An elevation is the most common view used to describe the external appearance of a building. Each elevation is labelled in relation to the compass direction it faces, for example, the north elevation of a building is the side that most closely faces the north. Buildings are rarely a simple rectangular shape in plan, so a typical elevation may show all the parts of the building that are seen from one particular direction.

- Sections: A section is also called a cross section. It represents a vertical plane cut through the object, in the same way as a floor plan is a horizontal section viewed from the top. The point where the section line is defined is shown on the elevations, usually with arrows pointing in the direction of the section view. Sections are used to describe the relationship between different levels of a building, and would usually have measurements such as storey heights, floor depths, and window heights shown.

- Site plan: This is a specific type of plan showing the whole context of a building or group of buildings. A site plan shows property boundaries and means of access to the site and nearby structures if they are relevant to the design. It may also need to show adjoining streets to demonstrate how the building fits into the local area. Within the site boundary, the site plan provides an overview of the entire scope of work. It shows the buildings already existing (if any) and those that are proposed, usually as a building footprint, in addition to surrounding roads, parking, footpaths, hard landscaping, trees and planting.

- The site plan also shows all the service connections: drainage and sewer lines, water supply, electrical and communications cables, exterior lighting and so on. Drainage chambers (manholes) are usually shown with a cover level (CL) and an invert level (IL). The invert is the bottom point of the pipe, so the different levels shown at individual chambers would dictate the fall required and the depth of the pipe below ground.

- Detail drawings: These drawings show a small part of the construction at a larger scale, to show how the component parts fit together. They are also used to show small surface details, for example, decorative elements. Section drawings in a large scale are a standard way of showing building construction details, typically showing complex junctions (such as floor to wall junction, window openings, eaves, and roof apex) that cannot be clearly shown in a drawing that includes the full height of the building. A full set of construction details needs to show plan details as well as vertical section details.

The architectural drawings will indicate any building regulation details, such as foundation, drainage, or other underground notes. They will also show internal elements, such as fire doors, smoke alarm positions, Regulation Part M (disabled access) requirements, and several others.

It will not actually show every scope of the works – that's where the schedule of work (SoW) comes in. In order to receive accurate quotations from contractors, a document literally spelling out the works involved, as a list, should be created.

This list should also incorporate certain specifications and details, and you cannot have too much information in a SoW, as just the architect's detail drawings are not enough for contractors to provide accurate quotations. The document should be looked upon as the kingpin of the whole build procedure.

Some may call it a scope of works, but scope or schedule, the object of the exercise is to create a document that gives clear, accurate lists of the works required. The document is in effect a directory of the works to be agreed between the client and the contractor, so it should have as much information regarding each item as possible, to avoid any ambiguity during the execution of works.

A schedule of work outlines the specific tasks that need to be completed in the construction process but can become quite complex as it must cross-refer to its supporting documents.

The schedule of work is also used on site by the contractor's workforce on a day-to-day basis to determine work required to be completed during construction. For use on site, the schedule of work and its accompanying documents must not only identify the materials and allow calculation of quantities involved, but also give precise instructions on where all the materials are to be used and how they are to be incorporated together. It should also set out an ordered arrangement of tasks to be carried out in the correct sequence, to achieve the desired end result.

The structural engineer (SE) will have produced drawings and details showing any steel beams, or he may have designed items such as roof components or floor structures that require design and calculating. Having said that, most block and beam companies will provide their own design and calcs, as will truss manufacturers if you are not using a loose cut roof.

The SE drawings primarily present the load-carrying members of a structure. They outline the size and types of materials to be used, as well as the general details for connections. They do not address architectural details such as surface finishes, partition walls, or mechanical systems. The structural drawings give information on the design of the building's structure to building control for review and agreement. They can also become part of any contract documents, which guide contractors in terms of detailing, fabricating, and installing parts of the structure.

All the aforementioned information will usually be in the form of floor plans with the relevant beams and other structural elements marked on with the appropriate sizes, in addition to detail drawings of beam junctions and items that require very specific details explained, such as beam connections.

Accompanying this will be a document providing the structural calculations and any further information, such as a bending schedule for any reinforcing bars that have to be incorporated in a reinforced floor slab or foundation.

If you have a topographical survey drawing, it will show the following:

- The contours of the ground and existing features on the surface of the site, or slightly above or below the earth's surface (i.e. trees, buildings, roads, manholes, utility poles, retaining walls, and so on) will be seen in the drawing. The purpose of the survey is to serve as a base map for the design; it would usually include details of the perimeter boundary lines.

- Topographical surveys relate to local Ordnance Survey 'Bench Marks', from which all ground contours are mapped. Therefore, information regarding surface and underground utilities, sewers, and so on, is all determined by these levels. Bench marks are taken from mean sea level, so the increase in the number shown on the map is representative of the increase upwards from sea level; this number is therefore higher. Such a survey is an accurate representation of the area showing all natural and manmade features with levels. Shown as level reference points, all elements including the property, land features, and physical boundary details are presented on a scaled survey drawing. The amount of detail included in a topographical survey depends on your requirements, but typically, the land survey will include the existing buildings and structures, boundary details, a grid of levels, ground surfaces, tree positions, drainage details, and service chamber cover positions. Additional details can be included, such as the features adjacent to the site or underground services.

- A topographical survey is useful to the architect and certain trades such as ground workers, to show and determine the actual site levels in relation to any proposed levels. They can therefore show how far up out of the ground one side of the building is in relation to the other, or say the height that the driveway needs to be.

- A base level or Datum will be shown, to which all other marked levels relate. This will be a static position, such as a manhole cover in the road, which will not be altered or moved during the course of the works.

Now, all of the above will have been created by professionals, who, in theory, should not only be familiar and comfortable with all aspects of their own individual element, but also that of the others. And so do you need to be, whether you are managing sub-contractors or employing a main contractor.

All of the above represent the components of your home, so you need to look at them, absorb the details, and learn them like a script.

Hopefully, the build will go to plan (literally), but in the case of tweaks and changes along the way, you will need to understand both what should be built, and also whom best to turn to if something changes or needs to be changed. There's no point spending two days trying to get hold of the architect who is on the golf course again, when it's the engineer you should be speaking to. (Actually, he is probably on a different golf course). So it is extremely important that you familiarise yourself with the relevant information.

Likewise, it will probably have been months since the Groundwork Co last looked at your drawings, having worked on several jobs since. So it will be your job to take him through his refresher course when he starts your job. You can only do that if you completely understand how to read and decipher details on drawings.

Or as my foot soldier Fergie used to say, 'Prepare for the worst and expect the best' (I think he got that off someone else!).

5

Health and Safety on Site

I thought hard about where to include this chapter, and I realised that the best place for it is before I tell you how to begin any work on site. Do not be tempted for a second to skip past this.

To some it might appear to be a rather tedious subject, and especially now with the recent changes to Construction Design Management (CDM) legislations, simply a necessary box to be ticked that might not make particularly interesting reading.

However, health and safety (H&S) on site is an extremely important subject, and one to be taken very seriously. Whilst Book 1 contains a chapter covering the legislative side of things, it does not discuss the practical side of H&S on site.

Let me make one thing perfectly clear: law or no law, if something goes wrong, the buck stops in one way or another for both the client and whoever is responsible for running the site.

Long before I was qualified to manage construction sites, as an apprentice chippy, I witnessed an accident on site involving a big diesel mixer, a 12-year-old lad, and his leg. Without going into gory details, the lad who lived next door to a new house I was working on had been allowed to come on site by the bricky's labourer. The lad was interested in the mortar mixing – the labourer left the mixer to attend to the bricky, and you can guess the rest. The lad did not actually lose his leg, but it took the fire brigade and ambulance the best part of two hours to get him released from the clutches of the mixer and off to hospital where he stayed for many weeks. I am quite sure that he has since always walked with a bad limp.

This was in the late seventies, where serious health and safety checks at this level (one off new build house) had not really been invented, but the event and shortcomings of H&S on site has stuck in my mind for best part of 40 years as a reminder.

Nowadays, the site would be closed down by both police and the Health & Safety Executive (HSE) – with just about anyone they could think of prosecuted ... and rightly so!

I am proud to be able to say that right up until I moved on from building contracting five years ago, apart from cuts and bruises, there was never a serious accident on any site that I had supervisory influence on.

Most of site H&S involves common sense, which is easier to obtain if you are used to working on site. I learned the hard way what it feels like to stand on a nail sticking up through a piece of batten lying on the floor, so I quite naturally home in on anything as such. Likewise, I have worked on some very dodgy scaffolds over the years and slipped through gaps in the boards, so I can spot such a deficiency at 50 paces.

However, you, dear reader, will more than likely have a fraction of the experience or experiences to call on as I have, so you will need to be very diligent indeed in what is probably one of the most dangerous arenas in the world.

Nowadays, on a construction site of any size, all people entering the site - from the tea boy up to the project manager - will have to undergo some form of health & safety awareness training, such as the Construction Skills Certification Scheme (CSCS), and be able to prove it. I truly believe that self-builders, in whatever form, should also undertake at least a basic awareness course. The internet is awash with such basic courses, and for perhaps £150 and a day of your time, these courses are probably the most valuable investments you could make for your project.

A typical course in H&S would provide knowledge on

- Individual responsibilities for their own safety and the safety of others

- Typical construction hazards and how these are controlled

- How everyone can help achieve better practical standards of safety on site

- Legal requirements and liabilities

- How to work at heights

- Manual handling

- Fire prevention

- Work equipment

- Occupational health

The irony is that a common sense approach to H&S on site does not really show a cost implication (unless something goes wrong), so with some fairly basic training you can go a long way in avoiding any potential problems without finding out the hard way.

In my opinion, when you are costing out the works, the price of training one or two people should be up there in the costing spreadsheet, in the site setup/welfare column.

I will not go into individual trade-specific hazards and potential consequences here, but in Part 2 where I write a chapter on each trade, I will try to highlight H&S issues that you would be wise to absorb.

However, from a legislation point of view, you – the client – will have ultimate responsibility. It is therefore important that you make some fairly easy to implement and police H&S rules:

1. Invest in personal protective equipment (PPE). This is your last line of defence should you come into contact with a hazard on site. Wear your hard hat, safety boots, and hi-viz vest as a minimum, along with any additional PPE required for the task being carried out. Now this may seem a very obvious element, but it is extremely easy to police.

2. Keep the site clean and tidy. Construction work is messy, so remember to keep all work areas tidy throughout to reduce the number of slip and trip hazards. My pet hate – the nail in the timber – is easily hidden under a flimsy cement bag cast aside, but it will bite you just as hard if you step on it. Pay particular attention to high-risk areas such as access and escape routes. When visiting a site, just the state of tidiness speaks volumes to me about how disciplined the site is.

3. Do not put yourself or others at risk. Everyone is responsible for their own behaviour. Construction sites are dangerous places to work. Make sure you remain safety aware. It is surprising how the behaviour of one person can affect another. Take the aforementioned example of leaving a nail in a piece of timber, then leaving it on the floor. You can guarantee that it will not be the perpetrator who stands on it.

4. Never allow people to work in unsafe areas. Make sure all work areas are safe. Don't allow anyone to work at height without suitable guardrails or other fall prevention equipment. Keep your eye on unsupported trenches. Make sure all have safe access. Don't allow work below crane loads or other dangerous operations. In theory, on a construction site, there are not many places that do not fall under this heading, so be mindful.

5. Report defects and near misses. If you notice a problem, don't ignore it – do something about it immediately. Encourage others to do the same; action cannot be taken quickly if management are not aware of the problem, and the sooner problems are resolved, the fewer the chances are for an accident to occur.

6. Never tamper with equipment. Never remove guardrails or scaffold ties. Do not remove anything! Do not attempt to fix defective equipment unless you are competent to do so. Do not ever tamper with equipment without authorisation. Someone removing an item of scaffold is the big wrongdoer here and needs firm policing.

7. Anything else that you can think of speaks for itself. Make whatever rules you see fit. It's your backside on the line!

You will be surprised as to just how easy these rules are to create and implement, good practices will also breed. Once all site operatives know that you run a tight ship regarding H&S and its rules, they will firstly respect it and also implement them.

Just remember to practice what you preach!

6

Extra Over Works

Let's address the subject of extra over works, or more accurately, changes to the originally priced works that can mean omissions as well as additions.

Now, if you are renovating or refurbing a property, it is almost inevitable that you will come across works that had not been anticipated and therefore not quoted for. To a small extent, this might apply to a new build, but it is nowhere near as likely, unless someone changes their mind, of course! If not considered correctly, the process of agreeing to extra works can literally make or break a job. Let me give you an example using a situation I encountered a couple of years ago.

A building contractor had been employed, with a Joint Contracts Tribunal (JCT) contract, to convert a listed old large house into apartments. There was a decent schedule of work prepared by the architect, and the main contractor was of a high calibre, the client a developer.

Halfway through the job, there was a major falling out, resulting in the builder throwing in the towel and me being asked to see the job through with a replacement builder. It transpired that numerous costly extra works were discovered whilst opening up and converting the structure. The architect had given a verbal agreement to the works, but no one had actually had the sense to put figures to the works, which mounted up significantly and quickly. The architect allowed the builder to draw down monies on a regular basis, until on one occasion, the builder presented the architect and client with a quantity surveyor (QS) priced account of the extra works totalling over £100k. The problem was that the architect had been grossly underestimating the costs along the way and led the client to believe that the running total of extra costs was £30-£40k. The builder had been including extra monies on his drawdowns, so when the developer refused to pay the extra £100k, it was too late, as the builder had already drawn most of this additional figure down alongside his originally agreed works.

The reality was that the extra figure was indeed justified. It also came to light that the builder had been pressured by the architect to agree to complete the original works for less than he was comfortable with, therefore leaving him no wiggle room. He had agreed to contract the works for under £800k, when it should really have been £900k+. The developer and architect did not allow any contingency fund, so everyone was left feeling hard done by. From this point onwards, it got very messy.

As far as the builder was concerned, the architect had agreed to the extra works as contract administrator, but the client was now refusing to pay for them, which technically broke the contract, so the builder pulled off site. However, he had in effect been paid enough to cover the works - technically, he was overdrawn on the contract sum, but so what!

As far as the client was concerned, the job was potentially going to cost a further £100k, so he refused an attempt at reconciliation, claiming that the builder had broken the contract by pulling off the job, which was sort of true, but ... sort of not! The architect was trying to cover his backside - he took sides with his client - so the job fell apart.

I was then asked to be involved by finding another building contractor but to closely monitor (closing the door after the horse has bolted?) the works from that point onwards. The rather comical side of this was that it cost the client an extra £100k for Builder #2 to complete the works - well, it would, wouldn't it, when someone is picking up the pieces of someone else's work? So the client would have been wiser to strike a deal with Builder #1 in the first place.

The works then took many months longer to complete, and the real shame came when just before completion, a burst water pipe flooded three of the apartments caused by - you guessed it - the transition between the two plumbing sub-contractors, the second obviously blaming the first. But who knows.

The job then took a further three months longer to complete with no possible redress on Builder #1. Since the moment Builder #2 started works, it released him from any obligation.

Who was at fault here? Well, to a certain extent, the builder, for not tightly documenting the escalating extra works, but mainly the architect working on behalf of the client, for letting the circumstances drift out of control. The builder and architect had worked together on numerous projects previously, so familiarity breeds complacency in this case.

There are several morals to this story:

- First, do not be tempted to squeeze the cost of the works to an unrealistic figure. If your quotes are leaning towards a certain figure, then listen. This is no time for wishful thinking.

- Second – especially when dealing with a listed building – allow a healthy contingency figure.

- Third, monitor very carefully, however tedious, all extra agreed works costs.

The level of works will dictate, to a certain extent, how elaborate the system needs to be to record and control the agreed extra works, and sometimes, the speed with which a situation arises and the works that need to be done can cloud the issue.

This is where your role as the PM kicks in – agree to a system with the contractor(s) that works and stick to it no matter how tedious. Record all agreements in some form, even if simple email instructions. You will be amazed how many people develop selective memory when money is involved.

Include as soon as possible, the agreed figure in your costing spreadsheet so a firm handle can be kept on your spend. Conversely, if an omission is agreed upon, then record it in exactly the same way – all changes to the agreed works are either additions or omissions and will be simple to account for if addressed ASAP after the agreement is made.

Keep to the simple disciplines above and happiness will reign throughout the job!

7

The Importance of Airtightness

Whilst I made reference to airtightness in my first book, this chapter addresses the concept and its importance within the construction process.

To many in the UK, the concept of 'airtightness' seems somehow alien and unwelcome. 'I don't want to live in a sealed box' is a typical response, or 'I always sleep with the windows open, so what's the point?' They fear that an airtight house will be an unhealthy one, full of stale smells and condensation. Indeed, the classic Victorian house was designed to be as air-leaky as possible in order to expel the coal smoke: with rattling sash windows, draughts through the floorboards and open fireplaces. This, we thought, was healthy. But thinking has changed.

Now, with the growing awareness of concepts such as PassivHaus and zero carbon homes, people are realising just how important airtightness is in low-energy houses.

In an airtight house, air quality has to be planned with airtight homes relying on whole-house ventilation systems. We thus have three essential elements to a low-energy home: lots of insulation, airtightness, and a whole-house ventilation system. The first won't work without the second; the second won't work without the third; and if you combine all three, you get a low-energy, comfortable home with good indoor air quality.

Accredited and Enhanced Construction Details (ACDs & ECDs) go into significant detailing as to how to incorporate airtightness and thermal bridging measures within the design, but it is important for you to understand its relevance.

Achieving a decent level of airtightness is important for the energy efficiency of dwellings and the comfort of occupants. The benefits of improved insulation levels and more energy-efficient heating systems are lost if warm air can leak out of a building and cold air can leak in. A mandatory requirement for airtightness has been set by the Building Regulations (for England and Wales, and Northern Ireland) to ensure that reasonable standards are being achieved, and it is compulsory to subject newly built dwellings to a pressure test in order to measure and confirm their airtightness on completion.

I recently had a meeting with a person who I consider to be the guru of all things energy performance in domestic construction: Sarah Jones of Expert Energy Ltd. We often work together and, without sounding like a nerd (apologies you nerds out there!), regularly discuss the concept versus practicalities and mechanics of the build of numerous construction performance models.

Anyway, Sarah demonstrated via her software that as far as heat loss is concerned, the difference between an airtightness test level of 7 and a level of 3[a], would reduce the heat loss of a building by a **third**. Where a lower level is achieved, the building is more airtight.

I will note that at 3, the building would need mechanical ventilation heat recovery (MVHR) in order to provide a good level of fresh air. That is covered in another chapter, and is not really what this chapter is about.

The result of an air permeability test is used in the SAP calculation to confirm that the rate of CO_2 emissions from a dwelling is less than the target needed to comply with the building regulations. To achieve a level of 3 is far from difficult, but look at the benefits!

So back to the airtightness measures that you need to be aware of – the important thinking here if you are addressing this issue for the first time is to firstly understand where the potential issues are and then how they can be avoided and included.

Changes to building regulations have now made airtightness an issue that cannot be ignored, and as we get ever-closer to the zero carbon homes of the future, extremely high standards will have to be achieved in all new homes. The key thinking is that airtightness has to be given close attention from the early stages of the design and throughout the construction phase. Air leakage paths, which are commonly found in dwellings, can be easily avoided by careful design and good-quality construction practice.

[a] $(m^3/(m^2.h)@50\ Pa)$ in other words, the quantity of air (in m^3) that leaks into or out of the dwelling per hour, divided by the internal area (in m^2) of the building fabric at 50 Pa, which these days is easily achievable and falls within the level used to get basic construction through building regs

See the figure below to identify where these paths may be.

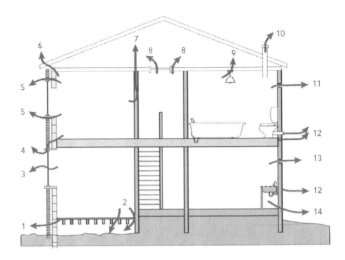

Air Leakage Paths

1. Suspended floors (timber and concrete beam and block):

    - Gaps between floorboards or concrete blocks around the perimeter of the floor and walls

    - Large gaps left around services that penetrate through the floor (for example, soil vent pipes)

2. Gaps left between floorboards or blocks; gaps around services (for example, pipes and cables)

3. Window/Door components:

    - Windows and doors that do not close tightly, providing air leakage paths (Note: You can have what in theory is a high-performing window with a very low U-value, but if the opening casement does not fit in its seal correctly, then air will leak and so will your valuable heat)

4. Joists that penetrate into wall construction:

   - Masonry walls: Gaps left around joists that penetrate across the inner leaf of external walls; air leakage from the cavity into the floor void, leaking into the dwelling through gaps between flooring and through any penetrations in the ceilings, for example, ceiling light

   - Timber frame construction: Gaps left around joists, which penetrate through the air barrier, allowing air leakage into the dwelling

5. Window sills and reveals:

   - Air leaks directly outside or into the cavity through gaps between the window frame and wall reveals

   - Inadequate seals to window casements

   - Gaps between doors and frames

   - Gap at bottom of door across threshold

6. Gaps between dry lining and ceilings:

   - Gaps and insufficient sealing at the wall to ceiling junction allowing air to leak into and out of the roof void

7. Internal partition walls:

   - Air leakage through internal partitions if the detailing or location of the air barrier leaves a pathway between indoors and outdoors; better to have plasterboard and membrane continuously across top of partition

8. Loft hatches:

   - Loft hatches that do not fit properly

9. Ceiling roses and recessed ceiling lights:

- Holes made through the upper ceiling for lights creating air leakage paths into the loft space

10. Gaps around soil and vent pipes and flue stacks:

- Gaps in ceilings around soil vent pipes and flue stacks allowing air leakage paths into roof void

11. Gaps around extractor fans and cooker hoods:

- Poorly fitted extractor fans and cooker hoods allowing air leakage through gaps left between the wall and the ventilation duct

12. Gaps around service pipes:

- Gaps left around service pipes, cables and ducts that pass through the dwelling's external fabric – a major contributor to poor airtightness

- Large holes often created for much smaller diameter pipes to pass through

- Gaps and holes around service penetrations often hidden from view behind baths, vanity units, and kitchen units

- Cuts and holes in vapour control membranes (used as air barrier for timber frame construction) made to accommodate pipes, cables, and ducts as they penetrate through

13. General air leakage through walls:

- Gaps in mortar joints (or in some cases missing mortar joints) between blocks on the inner leaf allowing significant air leakage from the cavity

- Cold external air drawn in through gaps and missing mortar joints in the blockwork wall behind the dry lining; draughts will be felt at the base of the wall (under skirting boards), through electric sockets, around light switches and light roses/recessed light fittings

The reasons for the air leakage may be the following:

- Gaps left around the service pipes

- Air barriers (vapour control membrane – timber frame or dry lining – steel frame) that have been cut to allow services to penetrate through the wall, creating air leakage paths into the dwelling

- Unnecessarily large cuts in membrane for service penetrations, making sealing difficult afterwards

- Use of the wrong tape to seal the membrane material; some tapes may not provide a robust seal and could peel off soon after being applied

14. Gaps between walls and solid ground floors:

- With timber frame, gaps left between the sole plate and the ground slab due to undulations in the concrete surface

Hopefully, you will have noticed from the list above that the first layer of defence is <u>inside</u> the fabric of the construction, with the cavity between the two skins of masonry or outside the timber frame being your worst enemy. Dry lining in the form of plasterboard 'glued' to the outside walls on dabs of adhesive are also a huge challenge, creating passageways behind the board for air to travel and leak through electric sockets and then through into the cavity. Wet plaster is by far a proactive measure, filling any gaps in blockwork joints along the way.

Once you understand where air leakage and therefore airtightness can occur, it is down to fairly straightforward mechanics and construction techniques to achieve the desired results.

The trick is to think it through carefully right at the beginning so you are always pre-empting the potential banana skins. Your biggest challenge is to educate and police the individual trades, the worst ones being the mechanical trades (plumbing and electrical), where you will particularly need your wits about you.

The best education on the subject that I ever received was when I experienced my first air test on a new building.

To perform the test, the front door is opened and replaced – temporarily – with an extractor door, which sucks air from the house, putting it under a small negative pressure load of 50 Pascals (Pa). This measures how much air is needed back in to keep the house at a steady 50 Pa. The negative pressure forms a draught at the points where the leak is effectively blowing onto your hand, helping you identify the leak.

The air leakage measurements are scored in cubic metres of air moving every hour through a square metre of the building envelope under 50 Pa of pressure, often shortened to just q50. It doesn't relate to what happens in practice, because homes aren't under pressure like this, but the figure does provide a useful way of comparing how leaky a house is. And, in practice, it also tells us how well a house has been designed and built. It's a sort of quality mark.

The key to getting a good score in an airtightness test is to design in an air barrier at the outset, and then to ensure that it is properly installed and not tampered with during construction. For instance, instead of allowing plumbers to drill holes wherever they like, the service connections need to be planned in advance and the air barrier penetrations sealed accordingly.

Likewise, the installation of windows and external doors, especially in masonry construction, must be well thought out using expanding tapes between the window and the structure and then sealing around the inner joint with airtight tape.

Unfortunately, for practical reasons, the air test is usually performed towards the end of the construction process, so by then, it is down to reactive measures to eradicate any problems rather than the proactive ones, which are best incorporated as the build progresses.

Timber frame has entirely different issues than masonry, so the thought process that you will need to ensure airtightness is equally different. However, the basics are the same – in fact, in theory a timber frame is easier to make airtight with modern membranes and tapes.

As I go through the individual trades elements in this book, I will try to point out as many potential issues on this subject in the relevant chapters.

8

Insulation

Quite a large aspect of the construction hinges around insulation, the reasons being two-fold – first, to insulate the fabric for thermal or acoustic reasons, and second, to provide a barrier either for air or moisture.

Insulations and Their Applications

Now, this book is not aimed at educating you on the different types of insulation and their properties per se – it would be far too involved for one chapter, and there are no doubt numerous publications on this ever-changing subject. I will, however, give you a brief overview on the types of insulation and their relevance in the construction mechanics without getting too deep and meaningful.

Insulation may be categorised by its composition (natural or synthetic materials), form (batts, blankets, loose-fill, spray foam, and panels), structural contribution (insulating concrete forms, structured panels [SIPs], and straw bales), functional mode (conductive, radiative, convective), resistance to heat transfer, environmental impact, and more. Sometimes, a thermally reflective surface called a radiant barrier is added to a material to reduce the transfer of heat through radiation as well as conduction. The choice of the material or combination of material used depends on a wide variety of factors.

There are insulations manufactured for suitability in masonry construction, and then there are insulations aimed more at the system build market, such as timber frame.

Consideration of Materials Used

Factors affecting the type and amount of insulation to use in a building include the following:

- Thermal conductivity

- Moisture sensitivity

- Compressive strength

- Ease of installation

- Durability – resistance to degradation from compression, moisture, decomposition, and so on

- Ease of replacement at end of life

- Cost effectiveness

- Toxicity

- Flammability

- Environmental impact and sustainability

Considerations about Building and Climate

- Average climatic conditions of the geographical area the building is located in

- The temperature the building is used at

Often a combination of materials is used to achieve an optimum solution, and various products combine different types of insulation into a single form.

Fiberglass Batts and Blankets (Glass wool)

Batts are pre-cut, whereas blankets are available in continuous rolls. Compressing the material reduces its effectiveness. Cutting it to accommodate electrical boxes and other obstructions allows air a free path to cross through the wall cavity. Blankets can cover joists and studs as well as the space between them.

Gaps between batts (bypasses) can become sites of air infiltration or condensation (both of which reduce the effectiveness of the insulation) and require strict attention during installation. By the same token, careful weatherization and installation of vapour barriers is required to ensure that the batts perform optimally.

Batts are typically used in cavities between walls and studwork. Blankets are used in roof spaces and between floor/ceiling voids.

Types

- Rock and slag wool: This is usually made from rock (basalt, diabase) or iron ore blast furnace slag; some rock wool contains recycled glass. It is non-flammable.

- Fiberglass: This is made from molten glass, usually with 20–30% recycled industrial waste and post-consumer content. It is non-flammable, except for the facing (if present). Sometimes, the manufacturer modifies the facing so that it is fire-resistant. Some fiberglass is unfaced, some is paper-faced with a thin layer of asphalt, and some is foil-faced. Paper-faced batts are vapour retarders, not vapour barriers. Foil-faced batts are vapour barriers. The vapour barrier must be installed toward the warm side.

- Plastic fibre: This material is usually made from recycled plastic. It does not cause irritation like fiberglass, but it is more difficult to cut than fiberglass. It is flammable, but it can be treated with fire-retardant.

Natural Fibre

Natural fibre insulations (similar to mineral fibre and fiberglass insulation at 0.04 W/mK), are usually treated with low toxicity fire and insect retardants. Natural fibre insulations can be used loose as granules or formed into flexible or semi-rigid panels and rigid panels using a binder (mostly synthetic, such as polyester, polyurethane, or polyolefin). The binder material can be new or recycled

Sheep's wool insulation

Sheep's wool insulation is a highly efficient thermal insulator with a higher performance than glass fibre and no reduction in performance even in the presence of condensation. It is made from the waste wool that the carpet and textile industries reject and is available in both rolls and batts for both thermal and acoustic insulation of housing and commercial buildings.

Wool has the ability to absorb significant levels of condensation – 40% of its own weight – and yet still be dry. As wool absorbs moisture, it heats up and therefore reduces the risk of condensation. It has the unique ability to absorb Volatile organic compound (VOC) gases, such as formaldehyde, nitrogen dioxide, and sulphur dioxide and lock them up permanently. Sheep's wool insulation has a long lifetime due to the natural crimp in the fibre – endurance testing has shown it has a life expectancy of over 100 years.

Wood fibre

Wood fibre insulation is available as loose fill, flexible batts, and rigid panels for all thermal and sound insulation uses. It can be used as internal insulation between studs, joists, or ceiling rafters, under timber floors to reduce sound transmittance against masonry walls. It can also be used externally using a rain screen cladding or roofing, or it can be directly plastered/rendered over timber rafters or studs, or masonry structures as external insulation to reduce thermal bridges. There are two manufacturing processes:

- Wet process: This process is similar to that of pulp mills, in which the fibres are softened, and under heat and pressure, the lignin in the fibres is used to create boards. The boards are limited to approximately 25 mm thickness; thicker boards are made by gluing (with modified starch or PVA wood glue). Additives such as latex or bitumen are added to increase water resistance.

- Dry process: In the dry process, a synthetic binder such as pet (polyester melted bond), polyolefin, or polyurethane is added and the boards/batts pressed to different densities to make flexible batts or rigid boards.

Cotton batts

Cotton insulation is increasing in popularity as an environmentally preferable option for insulation. It has an R-value roughly equivalent to the median value of fiberglass batts. The cotton is primarily recycled industrial scrap, providing a sustainability benefit. The batts do not use the toxic formaldehyde backing found in fiberglass, and the manufacture is nowhere near as energy-intensive as the mining and production process required for fiberglass. Boric acid is used as a flame retardant. A small quantity of polyolefin is melted as an adhesive to bind the product together (and is preferable to formaldehyde adhesives). Installation is similar to fiberglass, without the need for a respirator. However, some additional time is required to cut the material. As with any batt insulation, proper installation is important to ensure high-energy efficiency.

Advantages

- Cotton insulation has an R-Value equivalent to typical fiberglass batts.

- It is made from recycled content; it contains no formaldehyde or other toxic substances; and it has very low toxicity during manufacture (only from the polyolefin).

- The fibres do not cause itchiness; the airborne fibres do not carry a cancer risk.

Disadvantages

- Cotton batts are difficult to cut. Some installers may charge a slightly higher cost for installation as compared to other batts. This does not affect the effectiveness of the insulation, but may require choosing an installer more carefully, as any batt should be cut to fit the cavity well.

- Even with proper installation, batts do not completely seal the cavity against air movement (as with cellulose or expanding foam).

- The batts still require a vapour retarder or barrier (unlike cellulose).

- They may be hard to dry if a leak allows excessive moisture into the insulated cavity.

Loose-fill (Including Cellulose)

Loose-fill materials can be blown into attics, finished wall cavities, and hard-to-reach areas. They are ideal for these tasks because they conform to spaces and fill in the nooks and crannies. They can also be sprayed in place, usually with water-based adhesives. Many types are made of recycled materials (a type of cellulose) and are relatively inexpensive.

Advantages

- Cellulose insulation is environmentally preferable (80% recycled newspaper) and safe; it has a high recycled content and less risk to the installer than fiberglass (loose fill or batts).

- Loose fill insulation fills the wall cavity better than batts; wet-spray applications typically seal even better than dry-spray.

- It has a Class I fire safety rating.

- It does not contain formaldehyde-based binders.

- It is not made from petrochemicals nor chemicals with a high toxicity.

Disadvantages

- Its weight may cause ceilings to sag if the material is very heavy.

- Cellulose insulation settles over time, losing some of its effectiveness. Unscrupulous contractors may 'fluff' insulation using fewer bags than optimal for a desired R-value. Dry-spray (but not wet-spray) cellulose can settle 20% of its original volume. However, the expected settling is included in the stated R-Value. The dense-pack dry installation reduces settling and increases R-value.

- Air infiltration can significantly reduce effectiveness, particularly for fiberglass loose fill. Cellulose inhibits convection more effectively. In general, loose fill is seen as being better at reducing the presence of gaps in insulation than batts, as the cavity is sealed more carefully.

- It may absorb moisture.

Types

- Rock and slag wool: Also known as mineral wool or mineral fibre, rock and slag wool is made from rock (basalt, diabase), iron ore blast furnace slag, or recycled glass. It is non-flammable and more resistant to airflow than fiberglass. It clumps and loses effectiveness when moist or wet, but does not absorb much moisture, and regains effectiveness once dried.

- Cellulose insulation: Cellulose is denser and more resistant to airflow than fiberglass. Persistent moisture will weaken aluminium sulphate flame-retardants in cellulose. Dense-pack cellulose is highly resistant to air infiltration, and it is either installed into an open wall cavity using nets or temporary frames, or it is retrofitted into finished walls. However, dense-pack cellulose blocks but does not permanently seal bypasses in the way a closed-cell spray foam would. Furthermore, as with batts and blankets, warm, moist air will still pass through, unless there is a continuous near-perfect vapour barrier.

- Wet-spray cellulose insulation: This is similar to loose-fill insulation, but is applied with a small quantity of water to help the cellulose bind to the inside of open wall cavities, and to make the cellulose more resistant to settling. Spray application provides even better protection against air infiltration and improves wall rigidity. It also allows application on sloped walls, attics, and similar spaces. Wet-spray is best for new construction, as the wall must be allowed to dry completely before sealing with drywall (a moisture meter is recommended). Moist-spray (also called stabilised) cellulose uses less water to speed up drying time.

- Fiberglass: This is usually pink, yellow, or white. It loses effectiveness when moist or wet, but does not absorb much water. It is non-flammable.

- Natural insulations: These include granulated cork, hemp fibres, grains, all of which can be treated with a low toxicity fire and insect retardants.

- Vermiculite: This is generally grey or brown.

- Perlite: Perlite is generally white or yellow.

- Granulated cork: Cork is as good an insulator as foam. It does not absorb water, as it consists of closed cells. It resists fire and is commonly used in Europe.

- Others: Other types include cotton, wool, hemp, corncobs, straw, and other harvested natural materials. They are, however, not common.

Spray Foam

Spray foam is a type of insulation that is sprayed in place through a gun. Polyurethane and isocyanate foams are applied as a two-component mixture that comes together at the tip of a gun and forms expanding foam. Cementitious foam is applied in a similar manner, but it does not expand. Spray foam insulation is sprayed onto concrete slabs, into wall cavities of an unfinished wall, against the interior side of sheathing, or through holes drilled in sheathing or drywall into the wall cavity of a finished wall.

Advantages
- Spray foam blocks airflow by expanding and sealing off leaks, gaps, and penetrations (this can also keep out insects).

- It can serve as a semi-permeable vapour barrier with a better permeability rating than plastic sheeting vapour barriers and consequently reduce the build-up of moisture, which can cause mould growth.

- It can fill wall cavities in finished walls without taking the walls apart (as required with batts).

- Spray foam works well in tight spaces (like loose-fill).

- It provides acoustical insulation (like loose-fill).

- It expands while curing and filling bypasses, thus providing excellent resistance to air infiltration (unlike batts and blankets, which can leave bypasses and air pockets).

- It is superior to some types of loose-fill – wet-spray cellulose is comparable.

- It increases structural stability (unlike loose-fill, similar to wet-spray cellulose).

- It can be used in places where loose-fill cannot, such as between joists and rafters.

- It can be applied in small quantities.

- Cementitious foam is fireproof.

Disadvantages

- Cost can be high compared to traditional insulation.

- Most foams, with the exception of cementitious foams, release toxic fumes when they burn.

- Depending on usage and building regs, many foams require protection with a thermal barrier such as plasterboard on the interior of a house.

- This type of foam can shrink slightly while curing if not applied on a substrate heated to the manufacturer's recommended temperature.

- Although CFCs are no longer used, many use HCFCs or HFCs as blowing agents. Both are potent greenhouse gases, and HCFCs have some ozone depletion potential.

- Many foam insulations are made from petrochemicals and may be a concern for those seeking to reduce the use of fossil fuels and oil. However, some foams are becoming available that are made from renewable or recycled sources.

- R-value will diminish slightly with age, though the degradation of R-value stops once an equilibrium with the environment is reached. Even after this process, the stabilised R-value is very high.

- Most foams require protection from sunlight and solvents.

Advantages of closed-cell over open-cell foams

- Open-cell foam is porous, allowing water vapour and liquid water to penetrate the insulation. Closed-cell foam is non-porous and not moisture-penetrable, thereby effectively forming a semi-permeable vapour barrier.

- Closed-cell foams are superior insulators. While open-cell foams typically have R-values of 3–4 per inch (RSI 0.53 to RSI 0.70 per inch), closed-cell foams can attain R-values of 5–8 per inch (RSI 0.88 to RSI 1.41 per inch). This is important if space is limited, because it allows a thinner layer of insulation to be used. For example, a 1-inch layer of closed-cell foam provides about the same insulation factor as 2 inches of open-cell foam.

- Closed-cell foam is robust and structurally reinforces the insulated surface. By contrast, open-cell foam is soft when cured, with little structural strength.

- Open-cell foam requires trimming after installation, and disposal of the waste material. Unlike open-cell foam, closed-cell foam rarely requires any trimming, with little or no waste.

Advantages of open-cell over closed-cell foams

- Open cell foams allow timber to breathe.

- Open cell foams are incredibly effective as sound barriers, having about twice the sound resistance in normal frequency ranges than closed-cell foam.

- Open cell foams provide a better economical yield.

- Open cell foams often have a low exothermic reaction temperature; they will not harm coatings on electrical wiring, plumbing, or other building components.

Types

Icynene spray formula

Icynene uses water for its spray application instead of ozone-depleting chemicals. Icynene will expand up to 100 times it original size within the first 6 seconds of being applied. It fills all the tiny gaps around electrical sockets and hard to reach areas.

- Icynene spray foam insulation allows water to drain through it rather than storing it. Closed cell foams do not allow water to enter at all.

- Icynene is 100% water-blown. This means its chemical expansion is caused by the carbon dioxide generated between the water and isocyanate material. Icynene will not emit any harmful gases once cured.

- Unlike other spray foam insulation material, Icynene will not off gas over time. Icynene contains no ozone-depleting substances; it maintains its efficiency with no loss of R-Value through the life of the installation. This consistent R-Value and air barrier means energy savings are consistent throughout the life of the building, addition of further insulation will not be required, and

Icynene won't need upgrading in the future. The longevity of Icynene continues to reduce the impact on the environment for the future.

- Its flammability is relatively low.

- Icynene contains no chlorofluorocarbon (CFCs). Further, it contains no hydrofluorocarbons (HFCs) or hydrochlorofluorocarbons (HCFCs). Although HCFCs are better for the environment than CFCs, they still damage the ozone layer. These are not present in any Icynene product.

- Icynene contains no volatile organic compounds (VOCs). Many VOCs are dangerous to human health or cause harm to the environment.

- Icynene contains no traces of formaldehyde, a common building block for the synthesis of more complex compounds and materials. It is extremely toxic to many animals regardless of the method through which it is absorbed.

Closed-cell polyurethane
- This material is white or yellow. It may use a variety of blowing agents. It is resistant to water wicking and water vapour.

Open-cell (low-density) polyurethane
- This material is white or yellow. It expands to fill and seal cavities, but it expands slowly, preventing damage to the wall. It is fire resistant and resistant to water wicking, but permeable in terms of water vapour. Some types of polyurethane insulation are pourable.

Polystyrene (Expanded polystyrene [EPS] and extruded polystyrene [XPS])

- There are two types of rigid polystyrene foam plastic insulation, extruded (XPS foam), and expanded (EPS foam). Although both types of insulation are comprised of polystyrene, the two types of manufacturing processes produce finished products with very different performance properties. XPS is manufactured in a continuous extrusion process that produces a homogeneous closed cell crossed section, whereas EPS is manufactured by expanding spherical beads in a mold, using heat and pressure to fuse the beads together.

Insulating Concrete Forms

Insulating concrete forms (ICFs) are stay-in-place formwork made from insulating materials to build energy-efficient, cast-in-place, reinforced concrete walls.

Structural Insulated Panels

Structural insulated panels (SIPs), use the same concept as in foam-core external doors, but extend the concept to the entire house. They can be used for ceilings, floors, walls, and roofs. The panels usually consist of plywood, oriented strand board (OSB) sandwiched around a core consisting of expanded polystyrene, polyurethane, or polyisocyanurate. SIPs come in various thicknesses. In the process of building a house, they are glued together and secured with gussets of the same materials or timber studs. They provide the structural support, rather than the studs used in traditional timber framing.

Advantages

- SIPs are strong and able to bear loads, including external loads from precipitation and wind.

- Faster construction is possible with SIPs than in case of timber frame house. Houses built with SIPs also use less timber.

- This insulation type proves acoustical insulation.

- They are impermeable to moisture.

- Prefabricated SIP panels can be transported to site and be assembled on site.

- SIPs create a shell of solid insulation around house while reducing bypasses common to timber-frame constructions. The result is an inherently energy-efficient house.

- Formaldehyde, CFCs, or HCFCs are not used in manufacturing SIPs.

- SIPs offer true R-values and lower energy costs.

Disadvantages

- These insulation panels are more expensive than other types of insulation.

- They require thermal bridging at timber splines and fastening points, unless a thermally broken spline (gusset) is used.

Reflective Insulation and Radiant Barriers

Reflective insulation and radiant barriers reduce the radiation of heat to or from the surface of a material. Radiant barriers reflect radiant energy. A radiant barrier by itself will not affect heat conducted through the material by direct contact or heat transferred by moist air rising or convection. For this reason, trying to associate R-values with radiant barriers is difficult and inappropriate.

Reflective aluminium foil is the most common material used as a radiant barrier. It has no significant mass to absorb and retain heat. It also has very low emittance values or 'E-values' (typically 0.03 compared to 0.90 for most bulk insulation), which significantly reduces heat transfer by radiation.

Types of radiant barriers

- Foil or foil laminates

- Foil-faced polyurethane or foil-faced polyisocyanurate panels

- Foil-faced polystyrene – This laminated, high-density EPS is more flexible than rigid panels and works as a vapour barrier and thermal break; it is used in the underside of roof sheathing, ceilings, and on walls; for best results, it should not be used as a cavity fill type insulation

- Foil-faced plasterboard, also used as vapour barrier

- Foil-backed bubble pack – This is thin and more flexible than rigid panels; it works as a vapour barrier and resembles plastic bubble wrap with aluminium foil on both sides; it is often used on cold pipes, cold ducts, and the underside of roof sheathing

Radiant barriers can function as vapour barriers and serve both purposes with one product.
Materials with one shiny side (such as foil-faced plasterboard) must be positioned with the shiny side facing an air space to be effective. An aluminium foil radiant barrier can be placed either way – the shiny side is created by the rolling mill during the manufacturing process, and this does not affect the reflectivity of the foil material. As radiant barriers work by reflecting infrared energy, the aluminium foil would work just the same if both sides were dull.

Advantages

- Radiant barriers are highly effective in warmer climates.

- They show no change in thermal performance over time due to compaction, disintegration, or moisture absorption.

- Thin sheets take up lesser room than bulk insulation.

- They can act as vapour barriers.

- Radiant barriers are non-toxic and non-carcinogenic.

- They will not mould or mildew.

- The radon retarder in these barriers will limit radon penetration through the floor.

Disadvantages

- In very cold climates, radiant barriers must be combined with other types of insulation.

- They may pose an electrical safety hazard if the foil comes into contact with faulty electrical wiring.

9

Membranes

This is just a short chapter on the different membranes that you will come across during the build.

It goes without saying that the different membranes have to be built in to the works at the correct stage, especially with new areas, since generally they are covered up by floor and wall materials as works progress. It is therefore important for you to understand what they do so you can plan where and when they should be installed.

Membranes tend to be used for two things: to keep things such as moisture or gas out, or to keep things such as air/heat in.

To Keep Things Out

Moisture
Generally, damp proofing keeps moisture out of a building, where vapour barriers keep interior moisture from getting into walls.

A damp proof membrane (DPM) effectively functions as a moisture control barrier and will be used under/within the ground floor structure, quite likely as a polythene sheet acting as the moisture control to prevent moisture from passing into the interior spaces. The intention of linking the damp proof course (DPC) in the walls to the DPM under the floor is to seal the inside of the building from the damp, wet ground around it. In refurb work, if there is a problem due to the absence of a DPC or DPM, it is possible to install remedial damp proofing, but a professional damp survey by a certified surveyor in remedial treatment is essential to establish the exact cause of dampness in any property before action can be taken.

A DPM would also be incorporated within a tanking detail such as a basement and comes in several forms such as ethylene propylene diene terpolymer (EPDM), a material often used for swimming pools and flat roofs, bituminous and polymer modified 'paint on' membranes, and numerous impervious sheet materials which then rely on either a waterproof render or dry-lining.

Gas

Whilst there is a chapter dedicated to ground gas in Book 1, basically, there are two different types of gas that we are concerned with in a domestic build: methane and radon.

Assuming you have established which gas, if any, you need to treat, you must install the necessary membrane at the correct time, since fundamentally the application of each is very similar – usually just a different class of membrane is involved.

The idea is to seal across the ground floor to protect from below; more often than not, if you have a ground gas issue, with a new build, building a suspended floor such as block and beam would be prudent to allow ventilation of the void underneath.

Simply put, a special membrane appropriate to each gas has to be laid completely over the subfloor, lapping over and across the DPC level and cavity. The membrane can actually be used as a DPC, thus alleviating the need for an additional DPC. The membrane has to seal around any protrusions through the floor, such as drainage or ducting, so the timing of the installation could be an issue.

What I tend to do is ask Membrane Co to first lay the membrane around the perimeter and internal walls, just after the foundation stage and before superstructure works progress. I then allow all the major works to proceed and complete. Then immediately before the ground floor insulation and screed is laid, I have Membrane Co return and lay the remaining room areas, linking and sealing to the earlier laid perimeter. This eliminates the risk of damage to the membrane during works. Remember that it is more than likely that the inclusion of a gas membrane is a Building Regs issue, so it will need to be inspected before you cover it up.

To Keep Things In

Vapour control layer (VCL) or vapour control membrane (VCM)

A vapour control layer is a vapour-tight or a vapour-check membrane that is installed on the warm side (facing towards the liveable area) of a roof or on the inside of the exterior house wall. A key function of a VCL is to avoid moisture that builds up inside a house to find its way to the external wall and insulation material, which then absorbs the moisture and makes the insulation material lose its ability to insulate, thus allowing other condensation related issues to manifest.

A VCL is used extensively in timber frame construction for obvious reasons but also as part of Accredited Construction details on other forms of construction.

Introducing a decent level of VCL leads to the subject of airtightness and condensation, which has been covered in an earlier chapter.

There are several types of VCLs ranging from a basic polythene sheet to elaborate breathable membranes, each with different criteria according to the requirements.

To achieve a satisfactory level of airtightness and vapour control, vapour barrier membranes must be sealed at all laps, junctions, and penetrations. To reduce the risk of inadequate sealing, it is recommended that penetrations be kept to a minimum and services void be considered for electrical fittings, for example, sockets, light fittings, and so on, in front of the membrane. A services void can be created by spacing the internal lining (plasterboard) away from the vapour control and vapour barrier membranes. Timber battens with a minimum thickness of 25mm may be used for this.

For penetrations such as windows, doors, or pipework that cannot be addressed with a services void, careful attention must be paid to sealing. Those penetrations can be sealed with standard acrylic tape or flexible tape made of an elastic grade butyl adhesive. The advantages of these specialist tapes compared to conventional tape include faster installation, as fewer tape strips are required to be cut and applied and safer installation due to its flexibility, as the tape easily adapts to shapes and provides decent adhesion.

To ensure a good bond and tight sealing, it is crucial to press the tape firmly onto the membrane and to the item being sealed.

Repair all damages

Any accidental rips, tears, or perforations made in the membrane should be immediately repaired to avoid air leakage after installation. The damaged area may be repaired with tape, but extensive damage should be covered with an extra piece of membrane laid over the damage and sealed with tape.

The main thing to be borne in mind with all of the above membranes is that unless applied in one sheet (unlikely), the membrane is only as good as the effort to seal the joints, and the diligence of people working on or after its application to avoid/seal/repair penetrations.

10

CDM Obligations and Paperwork

The Construction Design and Management Regulations 2015 (CDM 2015) came into force on 6 April 2015, replacing CDM 2007.

Since the majority of you reading this book will be undertaking works that fall under the heading of 'Domestic Client' as far as the Health and Safety Executive (HSE) is concerned, we will focus our attention on this aspect of the legislation.

Below is a reasonably concise interpretation of the regulations that are likely to affect you. The list is not exhaustive, and you can find further explanation from the HSE.

Roles

A domestic client is any individual who has construction work carried out on their home or the home of a family member, which is **not** done as part of any business. While CDM 2015 places client duties on commercial clients in full, such duties for domestic clients normally pass to;

- The **contractor**, if it is a single contractor project, who must take on the legal duties of the client in addition to their own as contractor - in practice, this should involve little more than what they normally do in terms of managing H&S risks; and

- The **principal contractor**, for projects with more than one contractor, who must take on the legal duties of the client in addition to their own as principal contractor - if the domestic client has not appointed a principal contractor, the client duties must be carried out by the contractor in control of the construction work.

If a domestic client has appointed an architect (or other designer) on a project involving more than one contractor, they can ask them to manage the project and take on the client duties instead of the principal contractor. The designer then takes on the responsibilities of **principal designer** and must have a written agreement with the domestic client, confirming they have agreed (as principal designer) to take on the client duties as well as their own responsibilities.

Any designer in charge of coordinating and managing a project is assumed to be the principal designer. However, if they do not have a written agreement with the domestic client to confirm they are taking on the client duties, those duties automatically pass to the principal contractor.

Complying with CDM 2015 will help ensure that no one is harmed during the work, and that your building is safe to use and maintain. Effective planning will also help ensure that your work is well managed with fewer unexpected costs and problems.

Many clients, particularly those who only occasionally have construction work done, are not experts in construction work. Although you are not expected to actively manage or supervise the work yourself, you have a big influence over the way the work is carried out. Whatever the size of your project, you decide which designer and contractor will carry out the work, and how much money, time, and resources are available. The decisions you make have an impact on the health, safety, and welfare of workers and others affected by the work.

CDM 2015 is about choosing the right team and helping them to work together to ensure health and safety. As a client, you need to do the following:

1   Appoint the right people at the right time.

If more than one contractor will be involved, you will need to appoint (in writing) a principal designer and a principal contractor.

A principal designer is required to plan, manage, and coordinate the planning and design work. Appoint them as early as possible so that they can help you gather information about the project and ensure that the designers have done all they can to check that it can be built safely.

A principal contractor is required to plan, manage, and coordinate the construction work. Appoint them as early as possible so they are involved in discussions with the principal designer about the work.

Getting the right people for the right job means your designers and your contractors need to have the skills, knowledge, and experience to identify, reduce, and manage H&S risks. This is also the case if they are a company (known as having 'organisational capability' for the job). The designers and the contractors should be able to give references from previous clients for similar work and explain to you how they will achieve their given role.

2   Ensure there are arrangements in place to manage and organise the project.

The work is more likely to be done without harming anyone and on time if it is properly planned and managed. Sometimes the work is complex and uses many different trades. Often it involves high-risk work such as the work listed in the bulleted list below. The principal designer should understand these types of risks and try to avoid them when designing your project. The principal contractor or builder should manage the risks on site.

Following is a list of the biggest causes of accidents and ill health in construction work, and methods on how your designer and contractor can manage the risks by doing the following.

Falls from height:

- Make sure ladders are in good condition, at a 1:4 angle and tied or footed.

- Prevent people and materials falling from roofs, gable ends, working platforms and open edges using guardrails, midrails, and toeboards.

- Make sure fragile roof surfaces are covered, or secure working platforms with guard rails are used on or below the roof.

Collapse of excavations:

- Shore excavations; cover or barrier excavations to prevent people or vehicles from falling in.

Collapse of structures:

- Support structures (such as walls, beams, chimneybreasts, and roofs) with props.
- Ensure props are installed by a competent person.

Exposure to building dusts:

- Prevent dust by using wet cutting and vacuum extraction on tools.
- Use a vacuum cleaner rather than sweeping.
- Use a suitable, well-fitting mask.

Exposure to asbestos:

- Do not start work if it is suspected that asbestos may be present until a demolition/refurbishment survey has been carried out.

Electricity:

- Turn the electricity supply and other services off before drilling into walls.
- Do not use excavators or power tools near suspected buried services.

Protect members of the public, the client, and others: secure the site with net scaffolds and use rubbish chutes. Discuss how these risks are being managed with your designer and builder before work starts and throughout the build.

3 Allow adequate time.

Work that is rushed is likely to be unsafe and of poor quality. Allow enough time for the design, planning, and construction work to be undertaken properly.

4 Provide information to your designer and contractor.

Your designer and builder will need information about what you want built, and about the site and existing structures or hazards that may be present, such as asbestos, overhead cables, and buried services. Providing this information at an early stage will help them to plan, budget, and work around problems. Your principal designer can help you gather this information.

Putting together a Pre Construction Information (PCI) information document at the earliest stages, is a legal requirement. This pack includes as much information as you have about the project, along with the timescales and budget for the build, and how you expect the project to be managed, can help you to set the standards for managing H&S on site.

5 Communicate with your designer and building contractor.

Your project will only run efficiently if everyone involved in the work communicates, cooperates, and coordinates with each other.

During the design and planning stage, you, your designer, and your contractor need to discuss issues affecting what will be built, how it will be built, how it will be used and how it will be maintained when finished. This will avoid harm to people and unexpected costs because issues were not considered when design changes could still easily be made.

Meeting with your designer and contractor as the work progresses provides an opportunity to deal with problems that may arise and one to discuss H&S.

6 Ensure adequate welfare facilities on site.

Make sure that your contractor has made arrangements for the necessary and correct welfare facilities for their workers before the work starts.

7 Ensure a construction phase plan (CPP) is in place.

The principal contractor (or contractor if there is only one contractor) has to draw up a plan explaining how H&S risks will be managed. This should be proportionate to the scale of the work and associated risks, and you should not allow work to start on site until there is a plan.

8 Keep a health and safety file.

At the end of the build, the principal designer should give you an H&S file. If the principal designer leaves before the end of the project, the principal contractor should complete the file. It is a record of useful information, which will help you manage H&S risks during any future maintenance, repair, construction work, or demolition. You should keep the file, make it available to anyone who needs to alter or maintain the building, and update it if circumstances change.

9 Protect members of the public, including your employees.

If you are an employer (you are one if you have employed sub-contractors), or you have members of the public visiting your premises, you must ensure that they are protected from the risks of construction work.

Discuss with your designer and contractor how the construction work may affect how you run your business – for example, you may have to re-route pedestrian access, make sure the signs to your entrance are clear, or change the way your deliveries operate.

10   Notify construction projects to the Health & Safety Executive.

For some construction work (work lasting longer than 30 days with more than 20 workers working at the same time, or involving 500 person days of work), you need to notify the HSE of the project as soon as possible before construction work starts. In practice, you the client, may request someone else to submit the notification on your behalf.

Your principal designer or principal contractor will be able to advise you on your client duties.

If you do not comply with CDM 2015, you are likely to fail to influence the management of H&S on your project. This means that your project could be putting workers and others at risk of harm, and that the finished structure may not achieve good standards and offer value for money.

If you don't appoint a principal designer or principal contractor, you will be responsible for the things that they should have done. Serious breaches of H&S legislation on your construction project could result in construction work being stopped by HSE or your local authority, and additional work may be needed to put any issues right. In the most serious circumstances, you could be prosecuted.

11   There could be a Fee for Intervention.

HSE now recovers the costs of time spent dealing with material breaches of H&S law. This is known as Fee for Intervention (FFI). FFI applies when an inspector finds something wrong that they believe is serious enough for them to write to you about. A fee is charged for the time spent by the inspector in sorting out the issue. Following the simple guidance provided by HSE may help you to avoid having to pay a fee.

11

Insurances

There are several insurance policies that you will need in place for your build, all of them important:

- Building warranty

- Site insurance, including public liability and works in progress

- A combination of the above, and buildings insurance if working on an existing property

Building Warranty

Building warranty (BW), or to use its correct term, buildings structural defects warranty, is in effect an insurance policy put in place to protect the policy holder yet demonstrate compliance with correct construction methods. Like all other insurances, it is based on managing risk.

Although some insurers provide a product for refurb and conversion works, in the main, it is aimed at the new build. To warranty a conversion or refurb (unless under 10 years old) is a different kettle of fish for all concerned, with significantly more hoops to jump through, and therefore, it is more expensive for all concerned. With that in mind, the following is aimed at the new build constructor.

The usual term of a warranty is ten years, although I am aware of one company that will allow you to extend the period to twelve years. Think of it as another layer of building control, where as long as you are constructing correctly according to the design and the detailing, it is a relatively simple process to achieve – if you know what you are doing.

NHBC (National House Building Council) has long since been the representative of construction warranty and is the generic name for warranty providers in the same way that Hoover is for a vacuum cleaner. Up until about ten years ago, NHBC held the market with Zurich insurance for providing structural warranty. Indeed, it was always referred to as NHBC cover. As a building main contractor, I was a Zurich-registered builder with A1 status for 15 years, simply because I preferred working with them and appreciated their procedures towards the builder. Since I constructed most of my builds in one geographic area, I could build a relationship with the area surveyor on the basis of mutual respect for a high-quality build.

Clearly, Zurich saw the writing on the wall and decided to withdraw from the warranty side of their business at the same time as self-building exploded, bringing with it many other companies offering warranties.

Now there are some self-builders out there who are tempted to forego this ingredient of their build, and in my mind, this is at best unwise and at least a false economy.

Since the policy lasts for ten years, you may think that your plans to live in your dream home for many more years than that will negate the need for warranty, and so, save you on average £2000–£3000. However, it is entirely possible that your circumstances may change and leave you in the predicament of trying to sell an almost new build without an important ingredient.

The reality is that if you are turning to a lender to fund your build, it will be pretty well obligatory to put a warranty in place. Likewise, when someone goes to buy your house at some stage, their lender will insist on a warranty in place if the house is under ten years old.

Site Insurance including Public Liability and Works in Progress

Building your own home involves a lot of time, effort, and cash, so it's prudent to be prepared in case something goes wrong. For example, what if someone was injured on site, a storm damaged the construction, or valuable tools were stolen? It doesn't take much to throw the project off course and put you out of pocket. It is therefore essential to arrange appropriate self-build insurance cover.

A number of specialist insurers offer cover for self-build projects. Site insurance, sometimes called contract works insurance, covers a range of risks, including flood, storm, and fire, and usually includes any temporary buildings on the site, such as huts and caravans, as well as the property under construction. Also, more often than not, site insurance includes any professional fees, site clearance, and debris removal in the event of a claim.

When to take out the policy

Finding a site for your home-building project is just the first step on this highly rewarding path, but there will very likely be a time between your purchase of the land and the commencement of building works. As you are liable for any third parties that may enter your land, such as surveyors or ground technicians, site liability insurance cover would be an option if there is likely to be a significant gap between taking ownership and works commencing, and it will give the peace of mind you need during this time. The policy will cover you in the event that somebody is injured, or they have suffered damage or loss, whilst your plot is just a plot. Other than that, you would be wise to have the policy in place early doors.

What needs to be covered

When taking out the policy, you are usually be given the facility to opt in or out of certain elements, which will therefore affect the premium cost.

Contract works

This all-encompassing policy would usually last for 12–18 months and include employers' liability insurance, public liability insurance, and contractors' 'all-risks' protection – in short, all the insurance elements you need to feel secure while you're building your home.

Don't be fooled by the 'employers' liability' bit and think you do not need it. If you employ a sub-contractor, you become an employer.

Theft of equipment

Most self-build insurance policies pay out if thieves break into the site and steal any plant tools or equipment.

Site insurance will also normally cover any tools and personal effects belonging to employees, though there are agreed set limits. Of course, it's up to you to keep the site locked when not in use – and most insurers will insist on a decent level of security to deter potential thieves.

Hired-in plant

Although most plant hire companies will provide 'damage or theft liability' waiver, there is a cost to this that would quickly outweigh the figure for inclusion into your self-build policy. Once in place, you can show the document to Hire Co and not have to pay the waiver charge.

Responsibilities of the site owner

If you are building your own home, you have to think about protecting more than the site and its contents. You also have to consider your liabilities, both to members of the public and to your employees.

Let's say someone – even a trespasser – came onto site and injured themselves. Or maybe a falling branch damaged a neighbour's property. As the site owner, you could be held legally responsible, which means you could end up with a big compensation bill. A self-build insurance policy will typically cover public liability up to £5m, and you should make sure your policy is in place as soon as you buy the plot of land.

Employer's liability

As part of the CDM regulations, you also have a legal responsibility towards any employees, who could include self-employed tradesmen, employed by you for specific works, and you could therefore be liable to pay compensation, plus any costs, if they suffered an injury or contracted a disease as a result of working on the site. Check the limits on your policy, but most will include employer's liability up to £10m. Remember, this is obligatory!

Time scale

Self-build house insurance differs from a standard policy because it typically runs for 18 months instead of one year. There is also normally the option to extend the cover if the project is not completed on schedule. There are usually different policy structures for those intending to eventually live in the property as opposed to those selling it, so it is best to check the proposed cover when taking out the policy.

Surrounding property

It's worth checking that your policy covers any damage to surrounding property caused by collapse, subsidence, heave, vibration, weakening, removal of support, or lowering of ground water as a result of the works on your self-build project. Fundamentally, it depends on the nature of the works and the geology of the site. Your engineer or surveyor should be able to offer advice.

Renovation/Refurbishment/Extension Insurance

If you are undertaking works to an existing property, then you need to follow a different approach.

If you have just bought the property, chances are you have either not insured it yet or you have a straightforward building insurance policy. In the majority of cases, this will not cover you for the works or indeed the building whilst works are in progress.

If you are to commence works on your existing home, you cannot always rely on your existing household insurers to provide cover for the building works or provide cover for the materials on site and the additional public and employee's liability exposures. In almost all cases, you would be required to notify your present insurers that 'changes' are to take place. They may or may not then provide the cover whilst works are in progress.

Apart from the policy types mentioned previously, there are specifically designed insurances to cover your refurb project, whether it is a short period renovation or a larger extension project. These insurances can provide cover from three months duration onwards, but no matter what the duration of cover, you need to include all the new works, materials on site, public and employee's liability, as well as items of plant.

One last point on insurance – and it does not relate to policies that you need in place but more to those of others, especially professionals that you will employ.

All subbies should have as a minimum **public liability (PL) insurance**. Public liability insurance is a key cover for many businesses, as it can protect them and you if someone is injured or your property is damaged because of your business.

If the subbie has employees, contractors, casual workers, or temporary staff, he's required by law to take out employers' liability (EL) insurance. It'll cover claims from employees who've been injured or become seriously ill as a result of working for him.

Professional Indemnity (PI) Insurance

Professional indemnity insurance covers the cost of compensating clients for loss or damage resulting from negligent services or advice provided by a professional.

People such as architects, structural engineers, surveyors, and project managers all give advice in one form or another that if proved wrong could have costly and even disastrous results. If he (or she) is alleged to have provided inadequate advice, services, or designs to their client, PI insurance provides cover for the legal costs and expenses in defending the claim, as well as compensation payable to you, the self-builder, to rectify the mistake.

12

Inspections

There will be several times during the build that you will require certain works to be inspected by governing bodies such as building control (BC) (local authority or private), BW, or even certain incoming utility services. Let's take a look at each of them.

Building Control

The role of checking that building regulations are being complied with falls under the purview of building control bodies. There are two types: a local authority building control (LABC) service and a private sector approved inspector building control service. You are free to choose which type of building control body you use on your project.

In theory, the standard of the work they carry out should be to the same standard – the difference is more with regard to distance.

An LABC officer, as the name suggests, will work within a local authority area, perhaps covering a small part of that area and specialising in property type, such as residential. This means they will have excellent local knowledge and of local builders working in the area. Though it may mean the spectrum of work that they look at is limited, this depends upon the area and the building and property development activity in that area.

An approved inspector tends to deal with clients on a much wider geographical basis; therefore, they may not always have the flexibility of time that an LABC may have regarding appointments. At certain times of the project, the facility of telephoning and usually getting an inspection the same day can be very useful, especially in the ground (foundations) where it is not practical to have trenches left open overnight. You can do that with an LABC but rarely with private BC.

Having said that, private inspectors can sometimes be seen as being 'on side' while working with you. However, this must not be seen as an opportunity to get away with shortcuts. BC plays a very important role in the industry, and I would always recommend against using a private building control officer just to make your life easier. It is just as easy to do the works correctly in the first place.

There are voluntary performance standards in place for both BC bodies.

Below is a list of the different stages of work that should be notified to building control for subsequent inspection on site. Note that notification of commencement is necessary but does not necessarily provoke an inspection. A completion inspection is always necessary. Other stages of work should also be notified for inspection where appropriate or as agreed with BC.

Commencement

- Start of building work on the project or, for example, demolition of part of an existing property, site stripping, trial/exploratory works or 'setting out', with a view to beginning the building work thereafter

Excavations (Inspection)

- Any excavation, or work that relates to a future foundation of any part of a building before it is concreted (for example, trenches, bases, or other earth works for foundations, or reinforcement work, piling and other special foundation preparations)

Brickwork on foundations and damp-proof courses (Inspection)

- When foundation concrete has been placed into the approved excavations, 'raft', piling, or when other approved foundation preparations have been cast

- When DPC materials are to be placed on walls and/or floors (includes damp-proof membranes for floors) before being covered up

Oversite (Inspection)

- Preparation of the area underneath the building floor, prior to concreting or covering over (for example, 'hardcore', 'DPM', and/or floor insulation or subsoil under beam and block floors)

Drainage (Inspection)

- When drainage pipes and/or fittings for either surface, foul, combined or 'grey' water drains are being laid, and before they are covered (for example, 'soakaways', storm drains, foul drains, manholes, and inspection chambers)

Drainage test (Inspection)

- The testing of any drainage after it has been inspected and covered, and/or upon the completion work

Pre-plaster (Inspection)

- All structural and non-structural walls, floors, and roofs, and any associated insulation, prior to being covered by plaster / plaster boarding or other linings

Intermediate

- All other inspections not listed above, including general inspections of progress, requests for meetings on site to discuss problems or amendments of the proposals, re-starting of work following temporary halt or next phase of work, pre-commencement inspections or exploratory works and post-completion queries

Completion

- When building work has been done on the project prior to its occupation of the whole or part: the completed work should include all drainage, kitchen and bathroom fittings, and exit signage as appropriate but does not need to include decorations, furniture etc.

- Any outstanding conditions for structural calculations, sign off certs, and so on

Once satisfied, BC will issue a completion certificate.

A typical list of paperwork items to satisfy BC at sign off would be as follows:

- Structural calculations for block and beam floor
- Structural calculations for roof trusses, or entire structure if made of timber frame
- Part P electrical certificate
- Gas Safe certificate for all gas appliances
- Boiler and unvented cylinder commission certificate
- As built SAP calculation
- Energy performance certificate (EPC)
- Air leakage test certificate

Building Warranty

Subject to whom you use for your BW, it is entirely likely that the same company taking on the inspection/audit trail are also offering private building control. LABC warranty tends to use their own employed surveyors, but most other contract out the inspection process. Therefore, the surveyors/inspectors are qualified to the same extent for BC as they are for BW.

I personally, no matter what, prefer to keep the two separate using the 'two heads are better than one' theory.

Bearing in mind that essentially BW is about managing risk, their criteria for requirements from you differs from that of BC.

Usually the inspections and requirements for information and conformity in terms of BW are referred to as a site audit. Each stage that you are inspected at would result in a stage compliance certificate showing the stage you are at when inspected and any outstanding or new issues that require attention.

The stages at which inspection is required are usually very similar to those of BC, so in most cases, if you're satisfying BC, then you would be keeping BW happy also. However, again, since BW is concerned with risk, there are a few other items that the BW provider would be interested in in order to issue a final certificate:

- Building control completion certificate with confirmation that drains are tested

- Guarantee (insurance backed) for any flat roof coverings

- Guarantee (insurance backed) for any basement tanking

- Alternative heating appliance commissioning certification (PV panels, air/ground source heat pumps, and so on)

- HETAS (the official body recognised by Government to approve biomass and solid fuel heating appliances) certificate for any solid fuel appliances

- Mechanical ventilation air flow test certificate

- Natural slate declaration of conformity (EN:12326)

- Cavity ventilation on timber frame

- Mastic works

Utilities Inspector

Water

Unless you are using what is known as a TAP5 approved ground worker who can inspect and certify his own installation, you will need to have the water board come and inspect the new service pipe before it is covered up, in order to set an appointment for the connection and meter to be fixed at the road/boundary.

Most water boards will require you to have accepted the quote and paid for it before the inspection can be authorised. Thames Water, for example, require approximately five working days' notice to book the inspection, which can cause a bit of a logistics challenge on site.

I would not dream of suggesting that you contact the water board, tell them that the trench is excavated to the correct depth (min 750 mm), the pipe is in place surrounded by sand protection, the entry into the building is insulated and ducted with its stop valve on the end – when it is not really – and then await inspection just to organise the appointment. If you were then going to tell the above porky pies, you would perhaps do the above works the day before inspector is due, to avoid the obvious H&S risk or the trench caving in.

Some water boards – Affinity, for example – will allow photos of the aforementioned works to be sent to trigger the connection which, will allow you to backfill the trench straightaway.

13

Paying Your Bills

I know that we covered cash-flow and the concept of having your funds all worked out and in place in Book 1. We also discussed creating spreadsheets to record both the agreed prices and any monies paid. So in this chapter, we will address the mechanics and practicalities of paying the contractors and suppliers.

Let's make a couple of points clear here. First, construction workers, like most other people in the world, get up in the morning to put in a day's work with a view to getting paid for it. Second, if you become known for dragging your heels when it is time to pay, it will have a ripple effect on the works and therefore your programme. This is not some theory of mine – it is fact. You ask several tradesmen whom they are most likely to work for and give their best shot: the one who is slow to pay his bill or the one down the road who pays promptly. They will all chorus the same view. Likewise, who is most likely to squeeze a bit extra work out of a tradesman without a cost implication – the good payer? Of course!

You have agreed on the price and included it in your draw down spreadsheet (see Fig 2 below). You have also agreed on the payment intervals. Works have commenced and the subbie has completed an amount of the works. Therefore, he wants to apply for a draw (payment).

If all is in place correctly, his quote would have related to the schedule of work (see Book 1) with the individual items priced which are then placed on a spreadsheet created just for this contractor (see Fig 1 below). You will effectively have created a list of his agreed works with figures against them to be 'ticked off' and paid when completed. You will possibly agree to pay a percentage of a figure against an item as shown in the figure.

I prefer to keep figures on a net basis, whether or not the works will have a VAT implication. I find that it keeps things simpler - you may feel differently.

New Job				
Groundworks Co Draw summary				
S oW Item	Cost £	% drawn	Value to draw	Amount remaining
2.1.1	1440	50	£720.00	£720.00
2.1.2	2063	100	£2,063.00	£0.00
2.1.3	960	100	£960.00	£0.00
2.1.4	2615	0	£0.00	£2,615.00
2.2.1	4570	0	£0.00	£4,570.00
2.2.2	8245	40	£3,298.00	£4,947.00
2.2.3	1620	0	£0.00	£1,620.00
2.2.4	102	0	£0.00	£102.00
2.2.5	3340	100	£3,340.00	£0.00
2.2.6	750	0	£0.00	£750.00
2.2.7	2634	0	£0.00	£2,634.00
2.2.8	4320	100	£4,320.00	£0.00
2.2.9	534	0	£0.00	£534.00
2.2.10	534	100	£534.00	£0.00
2.2.11	1110	100	£1,110.00	£0.00
2.2.12	0	0	£0.00	£0.00
2.2.13	2240	0	£0.00	£2,240.00
2.2.14	3688	0	£0.00	£3,688.00
2.2.15	3007	0	£0.00	£3,007.00
extra depth founds	1850	100	£1,850.00	£0.00
Supply Toilet x 5	125	100	£125.00	£0.00
Total	45747		£18,320.00	£27,427.00

Fig 1 Trade Draw Summary

The totalled figure for his draw would then be transferred to the main draw down spreadsheet and show as a figure drawn against his total amount.

Draw down record

Trade	Amount Net	Additional works	Contractor	Draw 1 May	Remaining
Set up site/welfare/temp protect					
Groundworks inc drainage to DPC	£43,092.00		J Blogs	£18,320.00	£24,772.00
Block shell	£9,932.00		an other		£9,932.00
Timber Frame	£20,800.64	-£100.00	J Blogs	£16,000.00	£4,700.64
Scaffolding	£3,500.00		an other		£3,500.00
Roof coverings	£9,860.00		J Blogs		£9,860.00
Carpentry Works inc fascias & Windows	£25,164.00		an other		£25,164.00
Plastering inc associate works/floor screed	£13,651.72	£215.52	J Blogs		£13,867.24
Plumbing/heating	£16,400.00		an other		£16,400.00
Elect instalation	£7,641.00		J Blogs		£7,641.00
MVHR	£4,443.00		an other		£4,443.00
Kitchen install			J Blogs		£0.00
Finishings (tiling etc)			an other		£0.00
General attendance			J Blogs		£0.00
Decorate	£4,220.00		an other		£4,220.00
Mastic	£250.00		J Blogs		£250.00
Floor coverings			an other		£0.00
	#########				
Fees					
Management					
Engineer					
Building Control					
Architect					
Building Warranty					
Contingencies					
			Total draw	£34,320.00	
	#########				£124,749.88

Fig 2 Overall Draw Summary

You arrive at an agreed figure to be paid, and the subbie raises his invoice.

An aspect of your original agreement (mini contract – see Book 1) with him will be the payment terms. It may be 7 days, it may be 14 days, or it may be on receipt of invoice. Whatever you have agreed upon, make sure that you stick to it. You will be amazed at how quickly news travels between contractors that you pay your bills on time, and conversely if you do not. It has to be paid sometime, so might as well pay nice and quickly, and directly through the bank if possible. The days of issuing a cheque, putting it in the post, and then having the contractor wait for it to clear should be a thing of the past. You should create some form of cash-flow forecast to help you plan when monies will be needed to be available, so that it comes as no surprise that you need to part with your hard-earned money. Wipe the tear from your eye and hand it over.

Now on the subject of payment, there are only a few exceptions to any monies being paid in advance. A typical example would be for forward ordering of specific materials, for example, if the windows required for the construction have a long lead time are included in the contractor's package, but he has no credit facilities with Window Co. In this case, as part of a larger package with a contractor, the forward payment could be included in his invoice, but you should make the payment directly to the window company. Therefore, you will be in control of the finances but maintain responsibility with the contractor. Generally speaking, though, you should only employ a subbie who is financially self-supporting, and any contractor asking for 'monies upfront' speaks volumes about his credibility. Equally important is a client who is prepared to part with money before the subbie has anything to show for it, which sends out a message of compliance. You are then putting the subbie in charge of the proceedings and not yourself.

Retention

Another difficult and misconceived subject when employing subbies is that of a retention.

If you were to employ a main contractor with a formal contract, it is entirely likely (subject to the size of the works) that 5% will be deducted from each valuation. When practical completion is reached (at handover but with snagging items outstanding), half of the retention pot is released, and the other half (2.5%) held for an agreed defects period of usually six months to cover any defects and to give an incentive for the contractor to return and fix them.

Since this book has been written assuming you will employ sub-contractors, there are only a couple of trades where any form of retention could be argued as appropriate.

There is a small argument for retaining monies on a plumber, as leaks could manifest a week or two after final payment, or the boiler could pack up, but if you have chosen your plumber wisely, he will be the sort of person who stands behind his works after completion.

However, brickworks, for example, are either complete or not, and there is little about the works that could deteriorate once deemed satisfactory. Therefore, what would you be holding a retention for?

Whatever the trade you feel should offer some comfort by way of a retention, it is a subject that must be legally discussed, agreed upon, and put in writing at the time of acceptance, so that it forms part of your mini contract package. If you fail to do this, you would most definitely lose a battle in court if you withheld monies on the contractor without the retention agreed in writing.

If you do agree to a retention, make sure that you also agree to the terms.

Many years ago, I learned the hard way on this subject. A Plumbing Co that I was using for the first time (and last) had completed the works on a site of four houses that I was building. We had agreed upon a period of six months for the retention defects period, but soon after completion, we had a few problems that lasted most of the six months. I refused to release the retention monies because of the potential ongoing problems, the latest being only a few weeks before the end of the six month period, so the contractor took me through the small claims court.

The judge, whilst sympathising with my logic, ruled in favour of the contractor because we had agreed on a retention period of six months from completion, with no mention of facilitating any ongoing problems that could affect the agreed period.

The lesson learned is obvious: if you are going to agree on a retention, also agree on what will happen regarding the agreed period if you do have problems.

.

14

The Natives

Towards the end of Book 1, I touched upon the subject of neighbours and the value of keeping them on side.

Unless you are lucky enough to be building in the middle of a field, it is more than likely that you will need/want contact with the natives who can, on a whim, be your best friends or worst enemies.

The first signs of a construction site is being set up in the neighbourhood are likely to be greeted with dread. To many people, construction all too often means that their everyday lives are about to be disrupted by noise, dirt, early-morning deliveries, and vans full of under dressed, foul-mouthed, radio-blaring litter louts covered in tattoos and piercings, and with dirt under their fingernails!

However, believe me, you need the neighbours on your team, and with the right sort of mindset, you can make it work for all concerned.

There are a few reasons why you <u>need</u> agreeable contact with your neighbours:

- Party wall agreement
- Section 80 demolition notice
- Parking restrictions and deliveries

There are a few reasons why you <u>want</u> agreeable contact with them:

- Site security
- Information on positions of say buried services and drains
- Tolerance to site noise, dust, and so on

So let's say that you are about to commence works. The first thing I always do is write to the immediate neighbours – two or three each side, immediately opposite, and a few each side of them, and any to the rear. I introduce myself, explain what is being built/demolished/converted, and how long it should take. I go on to inform them that there will be very strict site rules regarding, amongst other things, nuisance to neighbours, and there will be public floggings – to which they could have front row seats – of anyone flaunting these rules. I explain that I will of course sleep with my personal phone at the bedside in case they need to discuss their thoughts in the middle of the night, and finally, I will send someone round every Saturday morning with flowers and to clean their car (and empty the dishwasher).

In other words, I creep 'cos it will pay dividends.

Assuming you have agreed upon any Party Wall stuff (see Book 1), you will need to keep on top of developments if you are building within three metres of the boundary. The reality is that if the native wanted to take you to task over this and be difficult, he (or she) could force you to employ a party wall surveyor at your expense to see the job through.

Therefore, an amicable relationship will avoid any troubled waters that could bring you stress and slow the job down.

One of the Section 80 demolition notice requirements is to inform the natives that demo works are about to commence. Now, whilst they cannot actually officially object to this (demolition is part of your planning approval), they can make your (or more importantly Demo Co's) life miserable if you have Local Authority Highways or the Department of Environment camped outside the site every ten minutes with their noise meter, making you wash the road on your hands and knees.

There will be times when, because you have a few people working on the site and not enough room for off street parking, subbie will park outside native's house. Of course, native will spring out there to inform you that he is expecting a delivery, his daughter, the district nurse, any minute, so the offending vehicle cannot possibly be left there. Needless to say, Waitrose doesn't turn up, his daughter lives in Norway, and he is as fit as a fiddle, but he needed a clear view of the site so he could speed dial local authority the moment anyone left the portaloo door open.

Naturally, there will be numerous times when you need unrestricted access opposite the site entrance for deliveries.

An aggrieved native can make life very difficult for you on that front by parking his Volvo on the road opposite then going out to walk his border terrier Alfie, even though there is plenty of room on his drive. (Waitrose are coming again and need the whole driveway to reverse down).

No doubt, officially, you should not commence works before 8:00 am, but it's the middle of summer and the brickies could do with getting cracking early to make use of the cooler early morning. Native will be on the phone demanding to fix a date for the flogging, even though he is an insomniac and always up at 5:30 am, taking Alfie for his morning constitutional, and bricky has not even fired up his mixer!

What about when Groundwork Co has spent most of the day trying to locate the sewer just outside the site, then found it by ripping it out, only for native to saunter over and inform you that he knew exactly where the pipe was because he stood and watched the contractors lay the pipe in 1983, and complained about the noise and mud on the road back then as well!

I am sure you are getting my drift by now – it would be a serious investment of your time to cuddle up to the locals. For the sake of having your plumber go round and fix native's tap washer or let him put his old bike frame in your skip, befriend him and the others, 'cos they can also be of value.

The same native sitting with his curtain strategically placed and his finger hovering over the local authority speed-dial button will also get the binoculars out if an unsavoury someone arrives on site late at night having a look round. Don't forget; he doesn't sleep a lot!

Also, that parcel you were expecting containing that important part, but know that no one will be on site to receive it, could maybe be dropped at native's house, couldn't it? Of course it could 'cos you are now best mates – 'The plumber did a wonderful job. Only took him 15 minutes!'

15

Site Management

Now in most domestic build cases, taking the construction route to become a site manager, you would have to work your way up to this role over many years. You would usually start as a trained tradesman, then perhaps a foreman or supervisor in your trade, then making your way up through management training of some form before being qualified to run the entire site from start to finish. This would allow you to learn and absorb the nitty gritty of construction-related issues over a long period of time, therefore giving you the practice and skill to run the complete job.

In more recent years, if you came to the role from a more academic route, then you would probably have surveying experience and an academic qualification in site management. However, I being old school feel that there is no substitute for experience at this build level.

From your perspective, project management and site management are probably much the same, and at the construction phase, they do link together to a large extent. However, site management is exactly that – managing the events at site level with the associated trials and tribulations.

The whole concept of self-building often means taking on the role of site manager, and you dear reader, probably intend to take on the role with none of most of the aforementioned experience ... So there's a challenge!

Let us look at what makes the site manager.

In the construction industry, site managers, often referred to as construction managers, site agents, or building managers, are responsible for the day-to-day running of a construction project on site. Site managers are required to keep within the timescale and budget of a project, and manage any delays or problems encountered on site during the works. Also involved in the role is the management of quality control, H&S checks, and the inspection of work carried out. Many site managers will be involved before site activity takes place, and are responsible for managing communications between all parties involved in the on-site development of the project.

But in your case, you are going to be the site manager! You will be directing the day-to-day operations, so do you have the necessary technical experience? Do you have the required managerial skills and programming knowhow? Do you have the ability to act quickly and calmly when problems occur and panic abounds? Those are a lot of questions, and they all need answering if the project is to be a success. It's good to be prepared in advance, but maintaining a healthy project is going to require the use of all of the aforementioned skills in the continuous reassessment of progress.

The site manager should knit the contractors' labour with the flow of materials. This keeps the whole project moving forward. The manager should also be able to motivate the labour force and develop a team spirit to make best use of everyone's talents and expertise. They must also be able to mediate between the various personalities in the team to ensure that friction is kept to a minimum. Managing a site is not about ordering people about and shouting, no matter how stressful the job may become, nor is it about panicking if something goes wrong (it will). A cool calm head needs to be maintained at all times.

This, however, does not mean ignoring problems in the hope that they will go away. An attribute often underestimated is the ability to communicate with operatives at 'site level' with the tools to comfortably interconnect, therefore gaining the respect of the man on site, and streamlining the production.

Before works commence, the site manager will have worked out a site logistics scheme that will include the following:

- Materials storage, so they are used from wherever they are placed
- Welfare and storage facilities
- Vehicles and parking
- Waste disposal locations
- Temporary utility services

While work is taking place, the site manager will monitor progress, oversee delivery of materials, carry out safety checks, and sort out any problems that could hold up work as they arise. A site manager will also liaise with architects, engineers, surveyors, and planners. He or she will also ensure that work complies with building regulations and H&S legislation as well as other legal requirements.

Unforeseen delays, changes to the original scope of work, and bad weather can all create havoc with a construction project timeline, but a good site manager has the skills and temperament to overcome such obstacles.

It is the responsibility of the site manager to make sure that the deadline for completing work is met, and as site manager, you will at least share some of the responsibility if someone on your site has an accident.

A good site manager is well organised, good at supervising and mentoring others, and able to keep an eye on several things happening all at once!

So, whilst all of the above may come across as a little officious, it is important to know that there are many strings to the site manager's bow, and the more you have and are aware of, the smoother the site will run, therefore making it more cost effective.

Another trait of a good site manager is to know where and whom to turn to for help. Is it the architect or the engineer that you call if you come across a design issue? Do you know where the nearest A&E is in case of an accident?

Of all the elements that you will be faced with, managing the site is without doubt the most challenging and underestimated. It is also a role that requires many years of experience, with both site procedures and the people involved.

By holding frequent site meetings throughout the course of a project, you also have the chance to provide status updates and discuss any delays, risks, or improvements. When you're proactively honest and transparent in your communication, you have room to put a Plan B in place, if needed, or the flexibility to make new decisions as you move toward the finish line.

Encouraging the tradesman or builder to be honest about a delay is a thousand times better than him making over-optimistic promises to deliver and then missing your deadline. People often get into hot water when they assume a tradesman, supplier, or even architect knows what you expect or even what you're talking about, so don't fall into the trap of assuming someone has the same understanding of a situation, project, deadline, or task that you do. You can avoid this pitfall by having a conversation in which you openly discuss what's expected and how it might be accomplished. Always leave plenty of opportunities for interaction, and remember that you are creating a team here where everyone has something to bring to the table.

Part 2 of this book explores all the trade elements in order, with their individual wants and needs, which should assist you in knitting together all of the above, so read on!

Part 2

Let's Get On With It

Tomorrow
is the busiest day of the week.

Trade Elements

This section of the book will look at the individual trade elements that will be found in the SoW document, and discuss what each one should provide, including what you need to be looking out for.

The words below will assume that you have had your quotes prepared and decided on the contractors. Nevertheless, I will comment on what you should be looking for with each element – including any trade-specific CDM elements that should be noted and noticed with each trade – to put your mind at rest that you have chosen wisely.

As mentioned at the beginning of this book, I am not trying to teach you how to mechanically do the works. My aim is to give you an insight into what each trade should be providing, so giving you the opportunity to police the works on site. However, reading this section could also give you valuable information when making your decisions regarding individual contractors, and make you sound like you know what you are talking about!

16

Setting up the Site

In Book 1, I addressed planning the logistics and layout of the site, but here we are now, actually setting up the site. So how do we go about it?

If you are demolishing an existing building to make way for your dream home, you will have served all the notices, disconnected the services, had all the surveys done, and so on, according to all the pre-construction elements.

We will also assume that you have organised your new or temporary incoming services – water and electricity.

Now there are numerous legislative aspects that you have to bear in mind. Whilst the following is aimed at all sizes of sites, you need to cherry pick the items pertinent to yours.

The first job is to set up fences or hoarding around the perimeter of the site and fix your health and safety signs on the fence. Signs outside the fence should include 'Construction Work in Progress' and 'All Visitors Must Report to Site Office.'

Signs inside the fence should introduce the site safety regulations and give specifications about emergency and first aid equipment.

Vehicles

The one person that you certainly do not want to upset at your local authority office is the highways officer.

In a new build with possibly contentious access (near a school or on a busy road), you will have been slapped with a planning condition requiring a Construction Method Statement to be created and submitted. This will have been insisted upon by the highways officer and subsequently been OK'd by him for the condition to be discharged. In a nutshell, you will have documented exactly how you plan to deal with the comings and goings of vehicles, including mud on road and parking.

Even if you did not have to provide a method statement, you would be well advised to treat this subject seriously; I have known sites be closed down by Highways for not sticking to the rules.

The law says that you must organise a construction site so that vehicles and pedestrians using site routes can move around safely. The routes need to be suitable for the persons or vehicles using them, in suitable positions and sufficient in number and size.

The term 'vehicles' includes cars, vans, lorries, low-loaders and mobile plant equipment, such as excavators, fork lift trucks, site dumpers, and so on.

Minimising vehicle movements

Good planning can help to minimise vehicle movement around a site, for example, organise deliveries to a programme so materials do not need to be moved about.

To limit the number of vehicles on site

- provide car and van parking for the workforce and visitors away from the work area;

- control entry to the work area; and

- plan storage areas so that delivery vehicles do not have to cross the site.

People on site

You as the employer should make sure that all workers are fit and competent to operate the vehicles, machines, and tools they use on site. Accidents can also occur when untrained or inexperienced workers drive construction vehicles without authority. Access to vehicles should be managed and people alerted to the risk.

Turning vehicles

The need for vehicles to reverse, especially out onto a highway, should be avoided where possible, as reversing is a major cause of fatal accidents.

Visibility

If vehicles reverse in areas where pedestrians cannot be excluded, the risk is elevated and visibility becomes a vital consideration.

The Public

Each year, two or three children die after gaining access to building sites, and many more are injured.

Other members of the public are seriously injured by;

- materials or tools falling outside the site boundary;
- falling into trenches; or
- being struck by moving plant and vehicles.

The client's pre-construction information should include;

- project boundaries;
- adjacent land use;
- access; and
- measures to exclude unauthorised people.

Managing Site Access

Site boundaries:
You need to define boundaries physically, where necessary, by suitable fencing. The type of fencing should reflect the nature of the site and its surroundings.
Determining the boundary is an important aspect of managing public risk. Typically, in populated areas, this will mean a high small-mesh fence or hoarding around the site.

Authorisation:
The principal contractor must take reasonable steps to prevent unauthorised people from accessing the site.
- People may be authorised to access the whole site or be restricted to certain areas.

- You must explain relevant site rules to authorised people and undertake any necessary site induction.

- You may need to supervise or accompany some authorised visitors while they are on site or visiting specific areas.

Hazards causing risk to the public

Many hazards have the potential to injure members of the public and visitors. Consider whether these hazards exist on your project, and how you will manage them.

Falling objects:
You must make sure objects do not fall outside the site boundary. On scaffolds, you can achieve this using toe-boards, brick guards, and netting.

Delivery and other site vehicles:
Make sure pedestrians cannot be struck by vehicles entering or leaving the site. Obstructing the pavement during deliveries may force pedestrians into the road, where they can be struck by other vehicles.

Scaffolding and other access equipment:
Prevent people outside the boundary being struck while the contractors are erecting, dismantling, and using scaffolding and other access equipment.

Storing and stacking materials:
You can reduce the risks associated with the storage of materials by storing them within the site perimeter, preferably in secure compounds or away from the perimeter fencing.

Openings and excavations:
People can be injured if they fall into excavations, manholes,

stairwells, or from open floor edges. You'll need to put up barriers around or covers on these areas.

Storage

The law says you must keep every part of your construction site in 'good order' and every place of work clean. The objective is to achieve what is usually called a good standard of 'housekeeping' across the site.

In addition, all contractors must plan, manage, and monitor their work so that it is carried out safely and without risks to health. This includes careful planning on how the site will be kept tidy and housekeeping actively managed.

Safe and efficient materials storage depends on good co-operation and co-ordination between everyone involved, including the client, contractors, suppliers, and the construction trades.

On all projects, the arrangements for materials storage should be discussed and agreed between contractors and the project client.

- **Storage areas:** Designate storage areas for plant, materials, waste, and flammable substances, for example, foam plastics, flammable liquids, and gases such as propane and hazardous substances such as pesticides and timber treatment chemicals.

- **Pedestrian routes:** Do not allow storage to 'spread' in an uncontrolled manner onto footpaths and other walkways. Do not store materials where they obstruct access routes or where they could interfere with emergency escape;

- **Flammable materials:** Such materials must be stored away from other materials and protected from accidental ignition.

- **Storage at height:** If materials are stored at a height, for example, on top of a container, make sure necessary guard rails are in place if people are likely to fall when stacking or collecting materials or equipment from these spots.

- **Tidiness:** Keep all storage areas tidy, whether in the main compound or on the site itself.

- **Deliveries:** Plan deliveries to keep the amount of materials on site to a minimum.

Waste Management

Although a chapter has been dedicated to this subject, there is other legislation governing the proper disposal of waste, ranging from low-risk waste through to hazardous waste. These laws are enforced by the Environment Agency (EA) and local authorities, so make provisions for this element at setup stage.

All waste produced can also present a real safety hazard to workers on site if it is not properly managed throughout the project.

- **Work areas:** Make clearing waste a priority for all trades. Check that everyone is aware of what is required and that it is being done.

- **Skips:** Waste materials need storing safely before their removal from the site, so make sure that you allow sufficient space for waste skips and bins.

Plan where the skips can be positioned and how often they will need to be collected.

- **Waste within buildings:** Consider waste generated inside the building, and whether you need to provide wheeled bins or chutes to dispose of this waste safely.

Admin

Again, although we have a chapter dedicated to CDM obligations and paperwork, it is worth mentioning here that there are a number of legal requirements concerning notifications, risk assessments, safety plans, examination reports, and so on, which must be also produced or submitted at this time.

Welfare

This is always a sticky point on a one-off domestic sized site, but as a minimum, you need to provide by law the following. Everyone who works on any site must have

- access to adequate toilet and washing facilities;

- a place for preparing and consuming refreshments; and

- a place to store and dry clothing and personal protective equipment.

Decisions and action on welfare facilities need to be taken at an early stage of project planning but implicated during site setup.

Toilets

Toilets should be suitable and sufficient, ventilated, and lit, and kept in a clean and orderly condition.

Washing facilities

Washing facilities must be provided so that workers can use them immediately after using the toilet or urinal, even if they are provided elsewhere. Most domestic size sites will be OK with portable facilities.

Further, general washing facilities must be suitable and sufficient, kept clean and orderly and with basins or sinks large enough for people to wash their face, hands, and forearms.

Drinking water

Drinking water must be provided or made available at readily accessible and suitable places.

Notifying the Neighbours

As a matter of course with all sites – new build or refurb – I write to the immediate natives introducing myself as point of contact and giving them as much general information regarding the proposed works and the duration of the likely disruption.

I explain that consideration for them is paramount, that there are strict site rules, that disturbance will be kept to a minimum, but that unfortunately, construction works are generally a bit noisy and dusty.

This simple act is usually well received, and it serves as an investment. If you are new to the plot, you can glean very important information from the neighbours, so being on side with them is an absolute must.

So ... Let's get on with it!

17

Demolition

A half-decent Demo Co more often than not will have his own plant (machines) and will arrive meaning business. He will want to get on site, pull the building over, separate it accordingly, put the waste into big skips or lorries, tidy up, and get the hell out of Dodge. A very large element of Demo Co's price will be on the waste disposal, so he will not have an endless figure in for the labour. Therefore, he will want the job done efficiently, which of course suits you and your programme.

From a health and safety point of view, this is a very challenging time of the job with all and sundry neighbours and others considering it a spectator sport. It will be your job to ensure that no one but Demo Co's people are allowed on site. In an ideal world, you will have erected a hoarding rather than say Heras fencing to demark the boundary, but of course, this is not always practical. Suffice to say, if you are likely to get a visit from authorities of some form, it will be at the demo stage.

Now let's assume for the sake of this chapter that you are

demolishing an existing building, or part of on, to make way for the construction of your new house.

My first words of advice would be .... **do not consider doing this yourself!**

Although on the face of it the works seem simple enough, there are a whole host of legislative and H&S hoops to jump through, which if not in place, will land you on the wrong side of Building Control (BC), the Department of Environment (DoE), the Health and Safety Executive (HSE), not to mention the police, to name but a few. There are very strict laws regarding waste carrier licences and landfill tax that dictate heavily what may or may not happen to the material when you have dropped the building, with, in some cases, the need for the site to be registered with the DoE.

Not only that, demolition in its basic form is an extremely dangerous aspect requiring expert and professional procedures. You might think that by perching yourself and a mate on ladders and removing the roof tiles yourself for re-use or even to sell will make or save you a few quid – but you would be thinking wrong. If the tiles have a value, it is far better to negotiate it with Demo Co when quoting than run the risk of hurting yourself or being prosecuted. Having said that, if you have items of value, such as a fireplace or that 200-year-old grand oak staircase, then clearly they are worth removing before handing the building over to Demo Co. Taking the bother to remove cable or copper pipe for its minuscule scrap value is, in my opinion, a complete waste of effort versus gain and you will certainly not save any money with Demo Co's quote by stripping out any of the interior yourself.

So, assuming that you have decided to take the sensible route and employed Demo Co, you will perhaps previously have agreed with them as to who will provide welfare facilities (portaloo?), but other than that, they should be self-sufficient. Bear in mind my comments in the VAT chapter of the previous book about reclaiming VAT on hired items and including things like toilet or container hire in someone's package.

To begin with, whoever actually razes the building to the ground would at the very least need to be armed with an asbestos survey, as mentioned in the previous book. All decent demo companies will insist on it, because as licensed waste carriers, they will have to tick certain boxes with the DoE and inform them about where they are disposing of the waste. It's not so much about identifying any asbestos, but more about proving its existence, and therefore what happens to it. In the event that no asbestos-based materials are found in the building, Demo Co would need to prove that as well, so there would be no question of any in the waste when taken away.

If, for example, a bat survey was specified at planning approval stage, the results and any subsequent action will be needed by Demo Co for their file. You will also have to provide them with the CDM Pre Construction Information (PCI) pack that we have covered in a different chapter on CDM.

In return, Demo Co will provide you with their risk assessment and method statement for your CDM construction phase plan. You or they will have sorted the Section 80 demolition notice with your local authority building control (LABC) (irrespective of you using LA or private BC for the build process), and in return, LA will have issued a Section 81 notice noting any restrictions.

Demo Co will want confirmation (often in writing) that all main utility services are disconnected. When all the above are in place, stand back!

Different-sized demolition companies have different ways of going forward. If they feel that any salvageable materials are involved, they will no doubt strip them out by hand, and in some cases, if the house was built using a valuable brick or roof tile that could be recycled in the reclaim market, then they too will be separated, cleaned, palleted, and taken away. This will of course have been taken into consideration at quoting stage, and I have known circumstances where Demo Co will take the building down at no cost in exchange for the salvageable materials – but that is rare!

In most cases though, a large machine – 20 tonnes or thereabouts with a hydraulic grab on the end – will simply pull the building over, separating the inert materials from the non-inert. Usually the inert is taken away in large lorries, whereas the non-inert is put in a large roll-on-roll-off skips for disposal, and that's where the documents mentioned above come in. Inert material is effectively earth or clean hardcore that can go straight to landfill; non-inert is the remaining mixed material.

Quite often, I would have agreed with them to track in some of the hardcore as a hard-standing area for deliveries or parking, which, especially if building a superstructure during the winter, will come in very handy later and cost no money.

You will expect them, as part of their brief, to be grubbing up and carting away all foundations and obsolete drainage, and then backfilling with rubble/finings and tracking in to compact.

In many cases, you will be rebuilding in a similar area, so the more you track in and compact the ground, the lesser is the likelihood of founds, when dug, becoming larger than you want or even caving in, with the obvious cost of extra concrete and so on.

Make sure that they leave the entire area flat and level before calling it completed.

Now on a slightly separate but related note, if you are doing any ground sculpting, or reducing or raising general ground levels, it is usually far more cost effective to have Demo Co include it within their package, as they will already have the plant on site. Likewise, if top soil is to be removed and put to one side, to be brought back later by landscapers, then get Demo Co to do it within their works. Remember, moving material about is cheaper for them than taking it away. One thing to consider with this aspect is that it happens very quickly. In most cases, I would expect a decent Demo Co to be in, drop and clear away a reasonably sized detached house; and be gone in a week or so.

18

Groundworks

Once again, a decent Groundwork Co will have his own plant, which is a good indication about the calibre of his work. Most people think that groundwork is a rough and ready aspect of the build, but they are wrong. Just because they use heavy materials at this stage on a rather large scale with an equally large plant, it does not mean that groundwork is the simplest part of the operation.

If you think about it, with the requirement for accurate levels (topography) and measurements on foundations, including setting out levels and falls for drainage, there is a lot of maths involved in what happens in the ground – with disastrous results if he gets it wrong. Keep this in mind when choosing Groundwork Co: mucky he might be but thick he should not!

From an H&S point of view, you have to obviously be mindful of plant and machinery; but perhaps not so obvious are open trenches. There are important guidelines regarding the shoring up of deep trenches that are too involved for me to visit in depth (pardon the pun) here, but you would be surprised at the amount of physical injury that can be inflicted if a trench caves in on someone. Search the internet for this if you need further convincing.

A decent Groundwork Co will not want to leave trenches of any depth (foundations) open overnight, especially in wet weather, but if there are, then your task becomes more challenging to stop anyone 'straying' on to the site and falling in a trench outside working hours.

On this note, don't be surprised if your eco survey showed the need for planks to be left up the side of overnight open trenches to allow any animals that may fall in the chance to get out.

Another H&S point worth noting is the harm that wet concrete can cause to exposed skin. Quite simply, the chemicals in concrete will burn severely, so it is considered a hazardous substance.

Groundwork Co will be expecting to turn up and find a level playing field. You will previously have agreed with him where he will set up camp and who will provide welfare and storage, but it is best for him to be self-sufficient as much as possible, for the same reasons as it is for Demo Co.

You will have provided him with all the necessary up-to-date drawings, the topo survey, soil reports, structural engineer's details, and any other useful information.

It is entirely likely that if Groundwork Co is employing an engineer to set the building out, then he will want the above drawings in drawing DWG (CAD) format, so be prepared – we will get to that in a minute.

If you have agreed with him to sort out the temporary water supply as per the chapter on incoming services in Book 1, you will need to do this at a very early stage. Likewise, if mains electricity is not yet installed, Groundwork Co needs to be informed.

I am going to digress for a while on the subject of what exactly is part of someone's agreed brief and what is not, and this applies right throughout the build. Say, for example, you did not think to include the actual connecting of the temporary water pipe to the water meter stopcock in Groundwork Co's package, but he turns up and you need it done. You could arrange for Plumbing Co to come and do the job, but I would simply ask Groundwork Co to connect it for you as a favour to avoid having to get Plumbing Co in just to do this very simple operation. Of course he will agree, because if he raises the subject of additional cost for such a small item at this early stage, then you have chosen the wrong Groundwork Co, and you should tell him so. However, I would think it highly unlikely that such an item would not be placed under the heading of 'swings and roundabouts', as mentioned in my chapter on Contractor Selection (Book 1). My point is, you are all working as a team with mutual benefits, so do not be afraid to raise the subject and get used to asking for this help without needing to take a deep breath or practising for an hour.

Right, so he has set up camp in roughly the areas that you designated on your site layout plan. Do not fret too much about him and your carefully thought out site layout plan; he should know what he is doing and so will not put anything in the way of him getting stuck into his works. Remember, shifting things around unnecessarily costs him money, so he will have his own plan and can be left to it – yours can kick in when he is finished. He will be clearing the site at the end of his stint anyway, but equally important is the fact that if something needs moving (container), he will have the plant to move it.

One of the first things he will do is set out the position of the building. Most groundwork contractors these days will employ the services of a surveying engineer to do this for them. The engineer will have previously loaded the information gleaned from the CAD drawings onto his laptop and will go about establishing the exact position of critical points with the aid of a super duper eye-wateringly expensive piece of kit that connects to a satellite via GPS.

Needless to say, this procedure is extremely accurate and avoids a lot of work with tape measures and string lines. Of course, subject to the size and shape of the building, this method is not always used by Groundwork Co, but perhaps it is something of interest that you might ask when discussing his employment?

Foundations

Foundations will next be dug and concreted according to any structural engineer's details or building control requirements. This subject (foundation depths) is probably the only one during the build where we have the unknown. You have probably asked Groundwork Co to quote based on a specified depth, but it is entirely possible that when the ground is opened up, especially following demo works, that the foundations need to be dug deeper or wider. You should have requested that he include a unit rate ($£$ per M^3) for the extra dig and concrete, and allowed a contingency in the costing. If extra depth is required, you need an arrangement in the form of photos, taken while waiting in the wings, as time could well be very important when digging and concreting. The trick here is for the concrete to be poured wherever possible the same day that the trenches are dug to avoid any trench side cave-ins. So careful planning of timing for building control and/or building warranty inspections is crucial. It is extremely important that you have agreed with Groundwork Co about who will organise these inspection visits, with ground workers inherently expecting someone else to take on this responsibility. Since this is probably the first time that any BC or BW surveyors will have visited the site, it is of paramount importance to get this right and not get off on the wrong foot, so check carefully how much notice each inspector will need. If you are using the LABC, you can usually organise an inspection on the same day if you call before 10:00 am, and that is why I prefer to use them. At this stage of the job, momentum is everything with getting out of the ground as quick as possible extremely important, especially when building in wet or cold periods. Having said that, private BC works almost as well with a bit more planning – they usually work alongside BW at this stage. Just remember to take lots of pics with simple tricks such as holding the tape measure or level staff in the trench and snapping it to indicate depths and so on.

Another simple little tip – make sure enough excavated material is left on site for backfilling once the founds and footings are constructed.

If you are using a piled foundation, there is not much for me to add here, as Piling Co is usually self-sufficient. However, subject to the type of piling rig, it is entirely possible that you will need to provide a concrete mat (approximately 50 mm thick) over the whole area for the rig to work on, which may not be included in Piling Co's price.

The other thing worth noting on piling is that it can get very messy both on and off site especially in wet months, so make sure you cater for cleaning the road, or you can expect the wrath of LA's finest highways inspector.

A quick digression on the pouring of concrete in cold conditions: without getting overly technical, it is very rare that conditions in the UK would prove prohibitive for pouring premix concrete in foundation trenches. This is because of sometimes-misunderstood ground temperatures that would keep the concrete from freezing during the relatively short period it takes for its initial curing process, and the temperature created by the chemical reaction of the cement content. This, coupled with the temperature that the air needs to have dropped to for damage to take place, makes potential harm very unlikely. If in doubt, most premix concrete providers would have information on their websites. If mixing and placing by hand, significantly more caution should be taken, but conditions would still need to be very severe to affect concrete below ground in a relatively recently excavated trench. Pouring and placing concrete above the ground, however, should be given different considerations and protections if the air temperature falls below freezing within hours of placing it. Rain on recently poured (a few hours until initial curing takes place) concrete will not really be of any serious detriment, but again, information can be found on concrete suppliers web-sites.

Construction of foundation walls would be the next job, including any entry points for services (water service pipe) or drainage.

Gas Membrane

It is entirely likely that you will have to include some form of gas membrane in the ground floor slab. In the UK, we are usually concerned with methane and radon, and each has its own requirements and membrane type. Suffice to say that this can be a specialist's area, and although you can have

Groundwork Co install it, I usually have a specialist Membrane Co come and do the job. I have included a more detailed explanation in the *Membranes* chapter.

Floor

Ground-bearing slab or block and beam suspended floor would follow, but at some time during this stage, depending which one, the next inspection from BC and BW would be required.

Couple of tips on block and beam – there has to be a DPC under the ends of the beams where they bear on the foundation. Do not let Groundwork Co be over-enthusiastic when cement grouting the blocks. You want the grout, which is usually spread with a broom, in between the blocks without huge lumps on top that will get in the way of laying insulation nice and flat later. Do not allow the beams to overhang into the cavity, and make sure that any cavity fill is well below (min 150 mm) the DPC, which sits under the beams.

Block and beam will need to be designed either by a structural engineer or in most cases by the company supplying them. This is a straightforward requirement, but make sure that you have received the design and calcs from Groundwork Co before you deem his work finished with final payment due. Do not be led into believing that you do not need them for any reason – you will need them for BC.

Drainage

Drainage works do not really need a lot of guidance from me, except that you need to make sure that the pipework has pea shingle all around (above and below), rather than just thrown on top. It is there to support the pipe, but is often be placed after the pipework is laid to the correct levels. Likewise, make sure that the chambers (manholes) are supported on a bed of concrete.

If you are installing a septic tank or bio-treatment plant, make sure you have done the necessary percolation tests to know the length of outfall pipes. If it is the type fed by electricity, then don't forget the duct for the cable.

If you are constructing soakaways for rainwater drainage, make sure they are designed to adequately do their job. A soakaway is actually a holding chamber for the collected rainwater from roofs, driveways, and so on, to be stored whilst it takes the required time to dissipate into the ground. The ground conditions, including water table depths, will have an effect on the size and structure of the soakaway. Sometimes, a soakaway is a simple hole dug in the ground and filled with hard-core, and contrary to popular belief, the job of the hard-core is to fill the hole with a honeycomb to allow water storage. It's not to soak up the water, so it's not so much the type of hard-core but the size of it with no finings (small dust) that is important. The hole is lined with a geo membrane to prevent it from being filled/clogged with the surrounding dirt; likewise a membrane is placed on the top. The object of the exercise is to keep the soakaway relatively clean inside.

In some instances, we would use a large perforated concrete ring with a concrete 'biscuit' top. The chamber would not require filling with anything as it is self-supporting. For the same reason, we would sometimes create the soakaway with purpose-made plastic crates, which interlock and form a hollow chamber. The hole would be lined and covered with a geo membrane. These are usually used where a large soakaway is required (poor permeability) and where filling it with hard-core would get more expensive.

As you can see, the size of the soakaways has to be calculated according to the amount of water going into them and the rate at which the water can dissipate into the ground. Obviously, the water will dissipate quicker in gravel-based ground than in clay. A soakaway can be too big, but you would not want it too small.

Services and Ducts

If part of Groundwork Co's brief is to lay provisions for the new incoming services, then have it done at this early stage. The water service pipe can be laid directly into the trench at a specific depth, and ducts for electricity and gas can be laid in the same trench but spaced apart in terms of height. Make sure that you use the correct duct for the job – it has to be a perforated yellow duct for gas and semi-ridged black duct for electric. If you are laying duct for telephone, it should be grey with cable telly green.

If it is not in a straight line, it is best to Groundwork Co to lay the gas pipe inside the duct as they go. The water pipe will need to be inspected, as mentioned in the *Inspections* chapter, but the other should not. It is best to check with the individual providers, though.

Any ducts laid for services and so on should have a strong draw cord in them and not just the thin one that comes with the coil. The thin draw cord is there to help you draw the stronger one through, and it will rot over time.

When Groundwork Co feel that they are finished, the site should be back to its correct levels around the building, clean and tidy with all their surplus materials and plant removed.

19

Superstructure – Masonry

There are substantial and significant differences between masonry construction and system builds such as timber frame.

If you choose masonry, your favourite wooden legged bricky (you need to have read the chapter on *Contractor Selection* in my first book, *The Self-Builders Guide to Project Management*) would be next on parade; if timber frame, then it would be the scaffolder.

We will address masonry first, then moving on to timber frame. I will incorporate scaffolding within each section accordingly.

Masonry Construction

A good bricky gang will usually be armed with two or sometimes even three trowels (bricklayers) per labourer.

This ratio is subject to whether or not there is a forklift or means of allowing the labourer to look after three as opposed to the usual two.

Once again, there is an element of maths involved in setting out the coursing, opening, internal wall positions, and so on, so your bricky needs a reasonable level of intelligence – don't expect too many to be uni grads though!

From an H&S perspective, bricklaying comes with it the inherent risk of working at heights and with machinery, and whilst PPE in the form of hard hats is often relaxed at domestic levels of the build, the common sense approach as mentioned in my H&S chapter should certainly be employed. Decent footwear is an absolute must – no flip-flops. To be fair, many subbie brickies will have worked on larger sites with very stringent regulations, so they should not be backward on the subject.

Also on H&S, although I will give scaffolding its own chapter, the scaffold, or more importantly its housekeeping, is a major consideration when you manage the site. I would love a pound for every time I have discovered that a bricky has moved a scaffold board or made a small adaption to a tube. This is a major no-no and an element that you should police regularly and stringently. Technically, scaffold should be signed off as checked every seven days, usually with what is called a Scaftag displayed on the actual scaffold structure.

So, on to the structure:

Let me tell you that without a shadow of doubt, the bricklayer is the prima donna of all trades on construction sites. It has been that way for donkey's years and stems back to when the bricky always used to be the site foreman with all the fringe benefits. Anyway, show me a bricky, and I will show you a miserable (even with two good legs) know-all, who insists on having everything his own way. Some of them occasionally smile and are even cheerful (on payday), but I truly believe that when going through the bricky training school they are picked for their miserable disposition. You have been warned!

Cynical? Moi?

Just to clarify, I was a formally trained carpenter in a previous life and never found it difficult to be happy. But because of my site management years, I have become well aware of how to deal with the fickle, immortal bricklayer.

With that firmly in mind, you would do well to try to second-guess his every requirement and start with the ground conditions around the building. He will expect a bowling green standard of levelling so that he can stack his bricks without the risk of them falling over, or risk tripping over and perhaps grazing his knee. We have covered the logistics of where to put everything, but the closer the bricks are, the (relatively) happier your bricky will be. Don't forget that it is entirely possible that the bricks, sand, and so on will be delivered before he gets there, so maybe consult with him in advance and avoid a tantrum. Whenever possible, when delivered, have the blocks stacked on the floor slab, so they can be loaded into their laying stacks more easily.

The type of cavity insulation being used will dictate whether the brick skin is laid before the blocks or vice versa. If cavity fill (dry therm or similar batts) is being used, the brickwork skin will go up first. If a rigid PUR board that still leaves part of the cavity open is being used, then the blockwork's inner skin will be constructed first so that the insulation can be fixed to it. Just pay attention to ensure that bricky keeps the cavity clean of mortar droppings, especially at the initial stage, where just the one skin is standing and the cavity below the DPC can get full, therefore bridging across the DPC.

There are a couple of other reasons for keeping the cavity clean of mortar, which tends to hold on the wall ties causing, first, potential damp penetration across the two skins, but second, cold bridging.

On the subjects of cold bridging, the importance of airtightness, and other higher level detailing performance, your average bricky may not always be familiar with them. So if you are building to the upper EPC/SAP numbers with say accredited or enhanced methods of construction, you might need to swot up on them and keep a wary eye.

To be serious for a second, ignorance on the subject is not necessarily intentional – the importance of performance is often about the bigger picture, so your bricky could well need educating. However, remember, it's your show and you dictate what details he conforms to. For the record, all of the instructions above and many more are simply good practice and should be incorporated anyway, but not all tradesmen are familiar with them, and old habits die hard.

So bricky gets up to the first scaffold lift, which needs to be choreographed to perfection to avoid bricky spitting his dummy out but also to maintain continuity; therefore, ask bricky nicely when he would need this and have Scaffold Co on notice.

On the subject of scaffolding, make sure all CDM requirements are being met here, as scaffolding is notoriously the worst element that can bring HSE breathing down your neck. It is so tempting to have a, shall we say not quite adequate, scaffold in place, especially on simple or smaller scaffold needs, but you have been warned!

I know we will flit about a bit with different trades, but before you know it, you will be ready for first floor joists and

Carpentry Co (see chapter on *Carpentry*).

If using a concrete floor (which has to be designed in the same way as the ground floor), you would more than likely have arranged a supply and fix of this as a separate entity. This is a specialist performance requiring craneage and carrying its own H&S obligations, such as a fall arrest system.

I am going to digress again on the subject of VAT here. With those of you electing to supply certain key materials yourself, it is entirely possible that you would in the case of a concrete floor, but be care full of this element and the VAT reclaim scheme. I had a situation a couple of years ago where the client provided the supply and fix (S&F) of the concrete floor planks but bought it through his merchant account, which of course showed VAT on the invoice. Since it was S&F, if he had bought directly from the floor plank company, they would not have added VAT (zero for new build domestic) but as he had bought through the merchant on his account, they had no mechanism for not charging VAT on their system, and thus added it. It does not really matter, as client could include this within his VAT reclaim scheme as with all the other merchant invoices, right? Wrong! And the VAT man picked it up because since it was S&F, it should not have shown VAT, so the client should have claimed it back from the merchant who technically was wrong to have charged it in the first place. I am sure you can guess how far he got with that, because for the same reasons, the merchant had no mechanism for refunding the wrongly charged VAT, which was paid over to the VAT man through their own VAT return anyway.

VAT Man - 1. Client - 0.

Anyway, back to the subject at hand.

Lintels are built as works proceed, which is straightforward in itself, but anything that bridges a cavity horizontally must have a cavity tray.

Now, a cavity tray is often formed by a wide piece of DPC, although proprietary ones can be bought. In its simplest form, a cavity tray is a gutter that collects any moisture that finds its way into the cavity (can be more than you think if you have particularly porous brick) and channels it out though 'weep hole' gaps in the face brickwork. Over a cavity-bridging lintel, the tray is built into the inside skin above the lintel height. It crosses the cavity at the downward angle of the lintel and is then laid on the outside flange of the lintel, where the weep holes are positioned.

Over lintels is one of many places that cavity trays are required. A rule of thumb is that if any moisture that finds its way into the cavity (and we are talking about very small amounts here), it must not be allowed to run down to a surface where the cavity is closed horizontally, such as the window/door head. The lintel is doing its job; the cavity tray does a different one. Another common place requiring cavity trays is where a lower pitched roof meets an external wall, where the outside wall above the roof becomes an inside wall below it.

The brick/block skin carries on, the scaffold is lifted, and before you know it, you are up to plate height, ready for the roof structure and Carpentry Co's next visit.

Bricky Co would then return after the main roof structure is pitched, to construct gables. These gables technically do not necessarily require insulation in the cavity if a cold roof (insulation at the first floor ceiling); however, it is a good idea to include it for as many reasons as not, and the cost is very small.

As the works approach this stage, although BC probably will not want to inspect, according to who you are using for warranty, they might arrive, often to inspect cavity insulation and closures around the windows, which are best installed as works proceed to protect the insulation.

Make sure also that your bricky is covering the cavities (even with scaffold boards) each night to prevent the insulation from becoming overly wet. On that subject, although most modern full-fill cavity batts can afford to get wet as they are designed to allow the moisture to drain out, it is simply good practice to avoid this, as wet batts could sag, leaving gaps for mortar droppings and cold bridging. I am not going to try and discuss all types of insulation in this chapter, but the most important thing to watch out for are spaces, no matter how small. See my note previously about your average bricky and his understanding of cold bridging.

After this, to all intents and purposes, bricky has finished the superstructure shell, and will then jump on the internal walls, if you have chosen masonry.

Internal masonry walls are usually built of block using differing type and strength according to your requirements. They are tied into the external walls either by bonding them in as the external block skin is built, or more than often these days, by using wall ties that are laid sticking out from the external wall, to be picked up later.

A few pointers on the masonry superstructure:

Mortar:
Make sure that bricky's labourer is gauging the mortar correctly in every single mix. It is a very simple discipline, and apart from the obvious reason of correct strength, the correct

measurement of mortar in every mix will also ensure a colour consistency that is an absolute must on face brickwork. Quite often, any discrepancies that stand out in the overall effect of brickwork are caused by different coloured mortar. Use a container (bucket) that can be laid off smooth, therefore giving an exact quantity, rather than a shovel, which of course does not. If it is, say, a 5:1 mix that is specified, then make it five buckets of sand and one bucket of cement. Some labourers might say, 'I always put 30 shovels of sand in the mixer with a bag of cement.' Mmmm! That's all very well (sort of) with a full gauge of mortar, but what about half a gauge and so on? Also, on the subject of mortar, decide right from the word go where you will get the sand from and stick to it for the entire job, which in the case you are buying loose (10 tonne loads?) you may have to think cleverly if, say, the works only need 12 tonne. Likewise, the make of the cement should also be the same throughout. Interchanging either will give you different coloured mortar that will stand out like a sore thumb once the scaffold is down and it is all dried out.

Obviously, if you are not using face brickwork but blocks for rendering, the aforementioned instructions are not so important.

Bricks:
A big no-no is to allow the bricks to get wet before they are laid, and to be fair, most brickies will be quite strict about this. Some harder bricks will hold the moisture more/longer than the softer ones, but wet bricks will make bricky's life harder in terms of keeping the mortar snots off. They will cause the mortar to take longer to 'go off' (cure/set), and therefore making bricky's life difficult when making the jointing look pretty.
A lot of bricks come in packs and are covered with polythene, but subject to how long they have stood in some merchant's

yard, they could still be wet inside the poly, which will actually hold the water and make matters worse.

It's very simple – as soon as the bricks are delivered, cover them up and keep them covered. You will even notice that bricky will cover them with 'spot boards' when they are stacked in their pile waiting to be laid.

Don't forget to build in any meter cabinets.

With the elect cabinet, you will build the 'hockey stick' into the cavity for the incoming cable to travel up. This is not allowed with gas meter cabinets, which are just the cabinet and no 'hockey stick'. Don't forget the cavity tray and weep holes!

Having said all this, building cabinets in most new build cases creates an issue with cold bridging, where the cabinet replaces the insulation depth. So, more often than not, these days I bring the elect cable and therefore the meter up inside the building/garage in a duct, and the gas in in a ground-based 'semi-concealed' cabinet to avoid the issue.

I know I am covering a lot in this chapter, but a couple of sentences on if you are planning to use re-claim materials such as bricks or roof tiles:

Allow a much larger percentage for wastage at both the estimating stage and the ordering stage, as there will firstly be a large number of breakages, and secondly, a portion of them that simply cannot be used 'cos Reclaim Materials Co will have slipped a number of sub-standard ones in the pallet/pile. Don't say I didn't warn you!

And lastly ... An old bricklayer that I worked with for many years had a favourite saying: 'Rome wasn't built in a day – but I wasn't on that job.' I think he nicked it off Brian Clough.

20

Superstructure – Timber Frame And System Build

Like all other matters in construction, there are good timber frame (TF) companies and there are not-so-good timber frame companies. You will have read by now that I have been actively involved in constructing timber frame since I was 16 years old, which is, ahem, *cough* years ago, so I and have built literally dozens and dozens, and I would like to consider myself pretty well-versed on the subject.

Generally speaking, putting aside the numerous types of TF structure, the main difference in cost and quality is the materials used (or not) and what you are getting as part of the package; for example, timber floor joists as opposed to I-joists or metal web joists.

Other than that, TF employs timber engineering and numerous methods and levels of insulation and airtightness according to your budget. They are all fundamentally erected in the same way using a gang of carpenters and labourers with usually a crane for certain stages.

From an H&S perspective, TF Co should provide you with their risk assessment and method statement for the entire procedure, including crane lifting, so apart from welfare facilities and a power supply, they should be self-sufficient on that front as well. Clearly, scaffold is an issue with what is effectively an open platform at times during the period that the frame goes up. Since the scaffolding is erected in its entirety before any TF works commence, the platform is open on the inside with no guardrail and needs to only be used by TF Co at the appropriate times.

I have enlisted the pros and cons of masonry versus the numerous methods of timber frame construction in Book 1. For the sake of this chapter, I will assume the timber frame construction has a brick/block outer skin. However, at construction phase, the fundamental difference is the order in which the trades take place, so let's explore this.

Scaffolding Co are first, prior to the arrival of TF Co, erecting the entire structure, with all lifts boarded out, as opposed to masonry, where one lift at a time is erected and boards are lifted each time .

Timber Frame Co will have provided you with a detail about where each lift should be and about the position of the scaffolding in relation to the footprint of the building. Scaffold is usually erected using standards (the main poles standing upright), transoms (the main poles linking side to side), and pudlocks (the short poles running front to back supporting the boards). Scaffold erected for Timber Frame Co, however, is there to provide working platforms usually one just before first-floor level and one about 600 mm or so down from the roof fascia line. Masonry scaffold would usually have the inside standard positioned one board away from the superstructure, with the pudlocks overhanging to support this one board.

Since our poor bricky will be working below and through the first lift, the inside standard on TF scaffold is positioned two boards away from the TF line. Thus, once the TF is erected, it is easy for the inner two boards to be removed and the pudlocks slid back so that bricky can work on up through and onto the first lift. Once up to this lift, the pudlocks are slid forwards and the boards put back for bricky to work on. As the brickwork proceeds, the actual height of this first lift is dropped as well, with the second lift being lowered in the same way after Roofing Co have used it.

Now all of the above may seem like an extremely long-winded explanation, but if worked out carefully, they can save you a lot of money in scaffolding. I have known situations where scaffold had to be completely dropped after TF and roof coverings and started again for brickworks because simple planning as above was not thought out.

The TF should be erected in a self-sufficient manner by Timber Frame Co, and whilst most will offer you the option to simply supply, and ask you to have Carpentry Co erect it, this is not at all a good idea, even if you think you can save a few quid. In the first place, you will have a VAT issue (only zero rated if supply and fix – see *VAT* chapter), but most importantly, you will leave yourself wide open to 'areas of responsibility' issues. No, get them to erect it and have complete ownership until it is completed to your satisfaction before they hand it over for you.

Because of my significant experience and knowledge of TF construction, I was recently contacted by a Mr & Mrs Self-Builder, asking me to just come to site on an ad hoc basis and snag with and for them the timber frame that had just been completed. I went through it with TF Co contracts manager, and since it had been erected by the frame manufacturer, there was no issue for anyone – when I found a few items that needed addressing. The items were swiftly rectified, the building handed over, and everyone was happy.

For Bricky Co, the obvious difference is that he is only laying the one outside skin and probably not including any insulation.

I am going to digress here again. Something to bear in mind when setting out the foundations with TF is that contrary to popular belief, it is entirely possible that the frame could end up overhanging the inside skin blockwork a taste. When setting out, I would always recommend giving the cavity an extra 10 mm all around below ground to give bricky a chance to stay on the outside skin foundation. On a similar vein, one area that TF erectors often slip is in keeping the outside panels upright. Imagine the panel over two storeys, leaning out by one degree – bricky could need to set his work out to compensate this lean and maintain his minimum cavity width. In extreme circumstances, leaning panels will also affect window reveals, where the window follows the panel trajectory and the brickwork is upright.

Since the TF construction is mainly a one-stop shop, they should, at the end of their works, offer you a finished article ready for roof coverings and brick skin. So subject to the type of frame provided and your own knowledge, you will be expected to formally accept the works. This is where it could get tricky for those of you with none or limited experience.

Now I am not suggesting that every one of you first-time TF builders give me a call to snag as above, but it would be a useful investment to have Carpentry Co do so, who would be carrying on from them with first and second fix works, to cast their eye over the construction for you.

The same goes for Roofing Co, who will be laying the roof tiles/slates. It's a rare occurrence that the TF chippies have thought of every single fixing required for the follow-on trades that form part of their brief. However, once they have gone, you could find yourself on the pointy end of daywork from Carpentry Co if works that should have been done by TF Co have been missed and Carpentry Co has to do them.

On that subject, make sure that you have previously done your homework on what is part of TF Co's brief and what Carpentry Co should need to include in their package. Typical items are pipe boxings or noggins for plasterboard on the inside.

When snagging at handover stage, make sure that any tears in the external membrane (there will be some!) are repaired and the cavity fire battens (usually around windows and at corners) are fixed.

Back to the brick/block outer skin: this is a very straightforward affair for bricky – one skin of brick or block, no insulation (usually), and very simple L-shaped lintels that are pinned back to the frame. Windows and external doors would have been installed before he gets there, so no setting out, and apart from a few slightly different details, nothing could be easier!

There will still be cavity trays and weep holes to install where the cavity is breached, but the difference with TF is that the tray (usually wide DPC) will need to be tucked behind the external breather membrane that is fixed to the TF. This will involve slicing the membrane horizontally, tucking the tray under it, and then stapling and taping the whole thing back to the timber frame. If done neatly, one will weather the other at the cut.

It is entirely possible that the windows will have been fitted with the outer face of the window flush with the outer face of the timber frame. This is to maintain the thermal envelope and to easily make it airtight (covered in the airtightness chapter). Up until recently, the trend would have been for the window frame to sit out, therefore closing the cavity. But there is no point spending the equivalent of six numbers and the bonus ball on high-performing windows and doors if you are then going to build in a cold bridge with this detail.

However, this then gives us a detail at the outside window reveals that needs careful thought, since there could then be a gap at this point between the outside skin and the timber frame. A decent detail is to return the brickwork back up against the frame, but this brings two considerations.

First, bricky will have cut bricks up the reveals, so he needs to be made aware of it at quoting stage. Second, you will need a vertical DPC at the point where the brick touches the timber frame.

Insulated Concrete Forms (ICF)

I am going to write a few paragraphs on ICFs, but in reality, there are books on the subject and several different manufacturers with their own ideas.

Insulated concrete forms are cast-in-situ concrete walls that are sandwiched between two layers of insulation material, usually expanded or extruded polystyrene. These systems are strong and energy efficient. Common applications of this method of construction are low-rise buildings, and they really come into their own in basements. Traditional finishes are applied to interior and exterior faces, so the buildings look similar to typical construction, although the walls are usually thicker.

The two insulating faces are separated by some type of connector or web. The ties that interconnect the two layers of insulated forming material can be plastic, metal, or additional projections of the insulation. The joints between individual forms can feature interlocking teeth or a tongue-and-groove configuration moulded into the forming material, or simple butt-jointed seams that are glued together. Once the forms are in place and braced, and the required reinforcement has been installed, concrete is pumped into the forms. Reinforcement in both directions maintains wall strength.

Almost any type of finish can be used with ICFs. Plasterboard remains the most common interior finish and is the most typical means of meeting any regs for a fire barrier over plastic foams surrounding living spaces. Exteriors are much more varied and depend on customer preference. Renders are applied over ICFs in a manner similar to other non-masonry systems. Internally, cables and so on are typically recessed into cut-outs in the foam after concrete has been placed.

A major appeal of ICFs is the potential for reducing energy used to heat and cool the building. Some estimates place savings at 20% or more. The walls can often have a far improved air tightness 10%–30% better than masonry.

ICF systems can also contain a decent amount of recycled material. Concrete can be made using supplementary cementing materials such as fly ash or slag to replace a portion of the cement. Aggregate can be recycled (crushed concrete) to reduce the need for virgin aggregate. Most steel for reinforcement is recycled. Some polystyrenes are recycled.

From a sustainability viewpoint, the reduced operating energy, reduction of CO_2, long service life, and use of local and recycled materials make ICF construction environmentally attractive.

From a construction point of view, although in theory it is straightforward, I would recommend using a dedicated ICF Co, as with all system builds there are tricks of the trade, especially when dealing with the concrete pour aspect of the works.

21

Scaffolding

Without doubt, the noisiest trade in the entire industry is the scaffolders, and I am not referring to the sound of the tubes clanging together. They shout – nay, holler – at one another to the extent that you would swear that they were all deaf, and if ever you were to personify the lairy, wolf-whistling construction worker, it would be a scaffolder.

I think it is because your average scaffolder could find himself going to several sites in a day, often in close contact with Mr and Mrs general public, their daughter, and sister, which appears to give them the god-given right to display gladiator levels of bravado, and the conviction that they should demonstrate their god-like bodies and film star looks at the drop of a hat.

Have you ever come across a shy scaffolder? I thought not!

Their training involves having the volume of their voices turned up along with learning the application of hair products and moisturiser.

The torn clothes and rough and ready nonchalant look was invented just for the bulging biceps brigade that is scaffolders. With a bit of luck, they have learned how to bolt a few tubes together as well!

Having said all that, scaffolders on the other hand do tend to be cheerful and overflowing with building site banter, which adds to the rich tapestry of the working day in construction.

From an H&S point of view, however, they are by far your biggest challenge. To be fair, since they have governing bodies in their own right, most scaffolders should be well versed in matters of health and safety, but there is a little bit of 'stand back' when they are on site tossing their tubes about like highlanders. And it is here that they sometimes need reigning in.

If you think about it, they are the very ones creating a platform, which once complete, is open to scrutiny at all levels, but until that point they are effectively working on an 'unsafe structure' that paradoxically would get you shut down if anyone else was standing on it.

When the scaffold is going up, the works are fairly organised, but when it is being struck, anyone in the immediate vicinity is quite literally taking their life in their own hands. Due to the force of nature (gravity), when the scaffold is going up the tubes cannot be thrown about per se, but during the striking procedure when the only way is down, there is a terrific temptation to launch tubes, clips, and boards rather than pass them down methodically. And that is where you need to police with a stern hand.

You also have to be very mindful of the damage to the recently completed structure as the scaffolding comes down, which happens usually at an alarming speed.

'Now you see it, now you don't' doesn't come anywhere close!

Scaffolding is based on engineering, so it is a requirement of the Work at Height Regulations 2005, which state that unless a scaffold is assembled to a generally recognised standard configuration for tube and fitting scaffolds, the scaffold should be designed by bespoke calculation, by a competent person, to ensure it will have adequate strength, rigidity, and stability while it is erected, used, and dismantled.

Take the scaffold that is wrapped either with protective sheeting or with a 'top hat' temporary roof on it. This structure is potentially subject to colossal forces, mainly from the wind, so it needs particular design considerations.

HSE Guidelines

According to the HSE, all scaffolding must be erected, dismantled, and altered in a safe manner. This is achieved by following the guidance provided by the National Access and Scaffolding Federation (NASC) in document SG4 titled 'Preventing falls in scaffolding' for tube and fitting scaffolds, or by following similar guidance provided by the manufacturers of system scaffolding.

At the start of the planning process (PCI pack as part of your CDM requirements), the user should supply relevant information to the scaffold contractor to ensure that an accurate and proper design process is followed. Typically, this information should include the following:

- Site location
- Period of time the scaffold is required to be in place
- Intended use

- Height and length and any critical dimensions that may affect the scaffold
- Number of boarded lifts
- Maximum working loads to be imposed and maximum number of people using the scaffold at any one time
- Type of access onto the scaffold, for example, staircase, ladder bay, external ladders
- Whether there is a requirement for sheeting, netting, or brick-guards
- Any specific requirements or provisions, for example, pedestrian walkway, restriction on tie locations, inclusion/provision for mechanical handling plant, such as hoist
- Nature of the ground conditions or supporting structures
- Information on the structure/building the scaffold will be erected against together with any relevant dimensions and drawings
- Any restrictions that may affect the erection, alteration, or dismantling process

Competence and supervision of scaffolding operatives

All employees should be competent for the type of scaffolding work they are undertaking and should have received appropriate training relevant to the type and complexity of scaffolding they are working on.

Employers must provide appropriate levels of supervision, taking into account the complexity of the work and the levels of training and competence of the scaffolders involved.

As a minimum requirement, every scaffold gang should contain a competent scaffolder who has received training for the type and complexity of the scaffold to be erected, altered, or dismantled.

Trainee scaffolders should always work under the direct supervision of a trained and competent scaffolder. Operatives are classified as 'trainees' until they complete the approved training and assessment required to be deemed competent.

Erection, alteration, and dismantling of all scaffolding structures (basic or complex) should be done under the direct supervision of a competent person. For complex structures, this would usually be an 'advanced scaffolder' or an individual who has received training in a specific type of system scaffold for the complexity of the configuration involved.

Scaffolding operatives should be up to date with the latest changes to safety guidance and good working practices within the scaffolding industry. Giving operatives job-specific pre-start briefings and regular toolbox talks is a good way of keeping them informed.

Scaffold inspection

It is the scaffold user/hirer's responsibility to ensure that all scaffolding has been inspected as follows:

- Following installation and before first use
- At an interval of no more than every 7 days thereafter
- Following any circumstances liable to jeopardise the safety of the installation, for example, high winds

All scaffolding inspection should be carried out by a competent person whose combination of knowledge, training, and experience is appropriate for the type and complexity of the scaffold. Competence may have been assessed under the Construction Industry Scaffolders Record Scheme (CISRS), or an individual may have received training in inspecting a specific type of system scaffold from a manufacturer/supplier.

A non-scaffolder who has attended a scaffold inspection course (for example, a site manager) could be deemed competent to inspect a basic scaffold structure.

The scaffold inspection report should note any defects or matters that could give rise to an H&S risk and any corrective actions taken, even when those actions are taken promptly, as this assists with the identification of any recurring problem.

Now your biggest issue with scaffolding once erected is some unauthorised person making changes or removing an item. If someone takes a couple of boards off the scaffold for any reason, therefore forming a 'trap', it is a serious matter that could get someone hurt – you would be surprised how often it happens.

What about the roof tiler who removes a guardrail so the forklift can land tiles/batten? In the first place, no one should be adjusting the scaffold, but you can guarantee that he will not put it back, with potentially life-changing results. Someone removes a ladder to be used elsewhere, or even uses it and puts it back, but does not secure it.

Understand what the scaffold has been designed for with respect to loading. A normal working platform, the scaffold is not designed to have a full pack of bricks or roof tiles landed on it; but you just see how many times this happens if you have forklift on site.

If you have, then arrange for Scaffold Co to erect a loading bay, which will be reinforced accordingly to take the weight and will have a hinged gate to allow pallets to be landed.

Another aspect of scaffold policing is to keep it clean and clear of obstacles. Clearly, the people who use it the most – brickies, roofing carpenters, roofers – are the main culprits who leave their debris on the working platform.

Make them clean it up very regularly, as there are all sorts of ramifications of not doing so. If you think about it, anyone working directly on the scaffold should, in theory, have both feet on it at all times. If you have to clamber over or around piles of rubbish, you have a good chance of slipping under, over, or through the guardrail.

The list goes on, but you need to be aware and understand the issues. It is no good expecting other people on site to do their own policing – the buck stops with you.

I mentioned in an earlier chapter on *Health and Safety* that I recommend all self-builders should seriously consider taking a safety awareness course. Well, if you did, a significant portion of the course would be dedicated to scaffolding and its potential issues.

Whilst, during the course of reading this book, you will notice a certain humour to my writing, on the subject of any H&S issues, I am nothing but serious.

Any project manager or site manager worth their salt, be it a professional or self-builder, would be wise to address this particular element of construction with a great deal of thought.

22

Housekeeping and Waste Management

If there is one area that is underestimated more often than not, and therefore not allowed for on the costing sheet, it is that of site housekeeping – in other words, keeping the site clean and tidy.

A clean site tells all sorts of people all sorts of information. If I have the need to go to a site that I do not have direct control over, I can tell at a glance what sort of workmanship and disciplines I will find just by how well organised and clean the site is. I am not the only one with such observations. You will be having visits from BW and BW (if it is a new build) inspectors/surveyors who, whether they make it known or not, will be impressed (or not!) by the professional approach to a clean and tidy site. This in turn will give said inspectors the confidence in your build capabilities. Believe me: been there, done that.

Heaven forbid if you have an impromptu visit from the HSE, who would always find some form of deficiency no matter how diligent you are on the subject. They will be impressed by a tightly run ship on the cleanliness front, which to them speaks volumes on your efforts to conform to H&S matters. Bear in mind that lurking below that cardboard packaging strewn on the floor could be a trap (hole) or even my pet hate – the nail sticking out from the piece of wood – just ready to do damage to someone.

However, someone has to do the cleaning up – and regularly – which can show a cost.

Whether or not you are refurbing or building from scratch, there will be a lot of waste and mess that needs clearing up, and you will be surprised how long this can take.

You may think that 'the trades will be responsible for clearing up their own mess', and to an extent that is true, but quite simply, they do not to any decent standard, and before you know it, the next trade is thinking 'I found it in s**t order so why should I bother'. Cleanliness breeds cleanliness, so the ideal thinking is to expect a trade to clean up, say, 50% of their mess, and you will have to take care of the rest.

The amount of waste to be cleaned up escalates as the job progresses. Clearly Demo Co will take care of everything, Groundwork Co will also to a large extent, but once the superstructure kicks in, whether it be masonry or timber frame, so does the challenge of keeping things tidy.

I would say that quite easily at the top of your nuisance list would be pallets; during the course of a decent size refurb or new build, you could find yourself on the receiving end of say thirty pallets that would fill a complete skip even when broken down.

Most contractors will expect the site to be taking care of waste disposal, although they would be expected to get the rubbish (or most of it) to the skip, and that includes the dreaded pallets.

The last thing you want to do is put pallets in their full form into skips; you are simply filling the expensive skip with fresh air. So someone has the task of cutting them up to take up less room, assuming that you cannot burn on site, which is more often than not the case. If you have to get rid of them by waste disposal, my advice is to do it as they become surplus, otherwise you end up with a huge pile of pallets taking up space, towards the end of the job. A few pallets placed on top of what is officially a full skip will help the problem, as they also give the skip driver a surface to secure the other contents. For the record, there are very few pallets delivered these days that have any form of value. If they did, you would be charged a deposit on them in the first place.

Anyway, back to the cleaning up:

Give some very serious thought to this at the costing / site logistics stage. Quite a lot of you will jump in with 'I can do this myself'. In theory you could, but will you have the time or the opportunity? A new build in full flow would take someone one or two hours a day or half a day a couple of times a week to clean, and you would not want to leave it any longer than that. Don't be tempted to get youngsters to do it. In the first place, unsupervised under 16s are not allowed on a construction site, and secondly, I guarantee that your kids, the next-door neighbour's young son, or your brother would not do it properly and get bored, leaving you back with the problem. Plan site housekeeping properly, as you would one of the trades at the early stages, and save yourself the ensuing issues later.

Clearly, quite a lot of the waste can be recycled: brick rubble and timber off-cuts are easy to recycle. Back in the days of the Code for Sustainable Homes, I received credits on the Considerate Constructors scheme for giving timber off-cuts to neighbours, therefore ticking the box for recycling and having less infill for the skips at the same time.

This brings me to the topic of waste management.

Waste Management

Different stages of the job have different waste requirements.

At the early stages, it is usually heavy materials that need disposing of, whereas at the later stages, there is a lot of packaging and mixed waste.

Sometimes, with the heavy inert waste (rubble, dirt that can be taken straight to landfill or the crusher), a grab lorry could be more cost effective. Generally speaking, a $14m^3$ grab lorry will cost the same as a $6m^3$ skip, so do the maths. It can be beneficial if you have the space to create a pile for such materials to be taken away in full loads. Just bear in mind that the load has to remain inert with no timber (even tree roots) or other non-inert materials mixed in, or the whole load will be charged for mixed waste, which gets extremely expensive. This is a better option for those of you refurbing since inevitably there will be larger quantities of rubble and dirt.

One item to be borne in mind is plasterboard off-cuts and gypsum waste; most skip companies nowadays will not want you putting such products in with general mixed waste, so subject to the size of your works, you may need to consider a dedicated mini skip for this.

Plasterboard has long been an issue in the waste industry with changes in EA rules and differing opinions from waste companies.

The position statement from the EA states the following:

The landfilling of gypsum and other high sulphate bearing wastes with biodegradable waste has been prohibited in England and Wales since July 2005.

Until April 2009, we had been taking a pragmatic view that separate disposal was not necessary where construction waste contained small amounts (up to 10%) sulphate.

This was a working guideline that we always planned to review in response to scientific research.

Research, Sulphate bearing waste: Determination of a concentration limit for separate disposal, confirmed that the relationship between sulphate in waste and the production of hydrogen sulphide gas is complex. It concluded that we cannot set a practicable limit for gypsum wastes so we revised our guidance to remove the 10% guideline value.

To understand this guideline better, skips with mixed waste are usually taken to a waste transfer station where the contents are – quite often by hand – literally separated into the different recyclable elements. The problem with plasterboard is that it breaks up into very small pieces, so separating it becomes very tedious for Waste Carrier Co. Thus, apart from maybe the odd few pieces right on the top of the load, it has to have a separate disposal method.

For these reasons, Skip Co must make sure that plasterboard is kept separate. Some will offer grab bags, which you can have alongside a skip for plasterboard. Likewise, some Skip Cos have not yet caught up with the legislation, but such companies are few and far between.

One subject mainly aimed at you refurbers is that of asbestos-based products and Skip Co. None will allow you to include any asbestos-related materials in a non-dedicated container, and this means anything that remotely looks like it may have asbestos in it. I have known circumstances where a waste carrier has brought the full skip back to site for a few bits of cement fibre roof sheeting to be removed, which involved the skip being totally emptied then refilled without the offending pieces.

Some local authority transfer stations (local tip) will allow domestic users to take relatively small amounts of asbestos-based products to them for disposal FOC. Otherwise, the larger skip companies will provide a dedicated skip (at a cost), but there are a few hoops to jump through to register the site with the DoE, which you can do yourself, but for a small charge (usually included in the skip price), Skip Co will do this for you.

A clean site is a happy site ... and we all want that now – don't we, boys and girls?

23

Carpentry

Now you may be surprised to hear that in my opinion, carpenters are the backbone of the entire construction procedure. They are the only trade that takes five years to complete a formal apprenticeship and also the only trade that comes into contact with, and therefore works alongside, all the other trades. On that basis, they must have a decent understanding of the workings of these other trades, to enable them to dovetail (pardon the pun) the entire build.

They are without doubt the best looking, most kind, generous and intelligent members of the construction fraternity, and because of this, more often than not, go on to some form of site management. In very rare cases, they may elevate to the heady heights of consultant project managers and authors. Show me an ugly carpenter and I will put money on the fact that he is not formally trained.

The downside is that they are sometimes branded as know-all, self-opinionated, arrogant individuals, but I have never really subscribed to that way of thinking!

Carpenters tend to be divided into two camps according to their training and preference; basically, you get chippies that prefer to work with larger timbers such as roofing, joisting, framing, studwork, and the like. Then you get chippies who are more at home with the fiddlier and prettier side of the trade, such as second fix items – door hanging, kitchen fitting, and such. They are almost two different trades these days with only the older tradesmen formally trained in all aspects (ahem!) comfortable with either.

Just a quick paragraph on the difference between a carpenter and a joiner:

You need something constructed using a wood-based material and you want the right person for the job. But do you search for 'carpenters' or 'joiners'? Is there any difference between a carpenter and joiner or are they different terms for the same craft? Although the term 'joiner' is sometimes a geographical generic term for a chippy, there is actually a significant difference.

In summary, a joiner usually makes the timber products that a carpenter fixes on site. So, for example, a joiner might be employed to make the doors, frames, and windows. Traditionally, joiners would 'join' wood in a workshop, whereas a carpenter would construct the building elements on site. Carpenters would install the products made by joiners, and construct features such as the roof, joisted floors, and studwork. It would also be a carpenter, perhaps with an element of joinery shop training, who would hang the doors and fix skirting boards and so on.

It is not true that the difference between a carpenter and joiner is in whether or not they use nails!

Carpentry and joinery can therefore be understood as different specialisms within the same craft. In practice, there is crossover between the two disciplines, with apprentices learning many of the same woodworking techniques.

A joinery-trained chippy will make a good second fixer, but not very good pitching the roof or building studwork – he would simply take too long. It is basically a different discipline with both materials and the tools required; however, both should be shown (almost equal) respect for their talents.

There are several stages to the carpentry works of a build:

- Joisting
- Roofing
- First fix
- Second fix
- Finishings

Floor Joisting

The installation of floor joists is subject to the type you are using, be it timber or engineered joists of some form.

Very briefly, timber joists are positioned and braced; then the next lift of external blockwork is built around and carries on above. The floor deck is often later laid at the first fix stage.

Engineered joists such as the I-joist or metal web joist are placed and temporarily braced.

Then the floor decking (usually film-protected chipboard) is fixed onto it straightaway to complete the structural integrity of the floor. The deck could be fixed to timber joists at this stage, or not, but they must be laid straightaway with engineered joists.

A rule of thumb here regarding the fixing method – chipboard sheet or other manmade sheet flooring should never be glued to a timber joist; it should be nailed or screwed down with the joints glued. Have you ever been on the ground floor of a fairly recently built house and heard the click-click-clicking noise as someone walks about on the floor above you? Chipboard glued to a timber joist is usually the reason, and it is not an uncommon mistake. Only glue an engineered decking (chipboard) to a manmade joist, never glue manmade to natural (timber) joist

A squeaking floor, however, is a different problem, and is mainly also associated with timber joists. Often, the deck is nailed down to the timber joist at a time when the timber joist has a high moisture content (it got wet). Then later, when everything dries out and the joist shrinks or twists a taste, the nail is left protruding very slightly, leaving enough room for the sheet deck to slide up and down on the nail, therefore making a squeaking noise when you walk on it. The trouble here is that the problem does not manifest until say the heating goes on, and therefore just before the floor coverings are laid. To go over the floor, fixing it down further lends you to the problem of potentially nailing through a pipe that was maybe laid several months previous, so keep this in mind and maybe mark all pipes on the floor deck at early doors!

On the other hand, with an engineered joist (I-joist) the floor decking must be glued with the correct adhesive (usually a PU glue) both to the joists and to each other. You are forming a structural platform with the joist and decking as one.

Waterproof decking in the form of moisture-resistant chipboard with a protective film must be used, and it is best not to nail this very often, or even not at all, so no squeaking!

Keep your eye on the airtightness at this stage – a decent way forward here is to use a polypropylene joist end cap, which you fit over the end of the joist (timber or engineered) and then build into the masonry, forming an airtight seal. I know that some would favour using joist hangars and not building in the joist, but I personally do not encourage this method, as it is sometimes difficult to keep the joist line entirely true and can also encourage twisting of the joist. I know that there is a school of thought for using joist hangars to avoid any cold bridging at the end of the joist, but it is miniscule, since timber is a very poor thermal bridge.

From an H&S point of view, whilst technically a fall arrest system should be in place, the majority of joisting works is conducted from the scaffold, so common sense must prevail here.

Roof Structure

Most roofs are triangular in shape. Forming a strong triangle is important in lots of types of roof designs, because it gives the roof its strength, with a roof also adding strength to the walls of the building.

The wall plates that the rafters sit on, and are fixed to, need to be perfectly square and level. To be square they must be parallel – the same distance apart at each end of the roof, and everywhere in between. From this, all other aspects take place.

Now there are fundamentally two ways of constructing a roof with masonry construction and timber frame – loose cut and trusses.

This inevitably involves Carpentry Co, but equally inevitably, as with joisting, it will involve a different tradesman for the internal carpentry works.

Therefore, the chippies who pitch up to construct your roof will have their van full of tools, which would not be of much use to a scribe on a skirting board; however, they should be very good at maths, since roofing involves several angles, degrees of pitch, and calculations.

A loose cut roof involves a huge heap of timber, a talented carpenter, and more often than not, a steel beam or three – but I am not going to go into the different components such as rafters, hips, valleys, and ridges. What I will mention is that a loose cut roof takes longer to cut and erect than a trussed roof, and each will need different scaffold requirements that need to be discussed with Carpentry Co.

In the case of the loose cut, chippy will require a decent size area at his disposal to work his magic. A good one will take certain measurements then cut all the components using a circular saw, an adjustable square, and maths (trigonometry). He will then pass them up to his mate and hey, presto! It will fit.

Apart from the external scaffolding, some form of internal fall arrest (safety netting or bags of air or soft material usually) will be required in any case, and they can either be provided by you or written into Carpentry Co's brief. Bearing in mind the VAT element as discussed earlier, it is best provided by Carpentry Co to keep things neat.

However, from a CDM perspective, even though Carpentry Co might provide fall arrest, you are ultimately responsible as the client, so do not be thinking that if he chooses to work without it, it is his problem if some accident happens.

You could not be more wrong!

A common way around this is to have Scaffold Co erect what is termed as a 'birdcage lift' (don't know why it is called that). It involves completely scaffolding and boarding out the entire area just below the ceiling joist level and kills two birds with one stone. First, it provides fall arrest; second, it also gives roofing chippy a good working platform to fix the many roof components.

If the structure has gables, Carpentry Co constructs certain roofing elements. Bricky comes back and builds the gables. Then Carpentry Co builds some more with a dash of Scaffolder Co in the mix for good measure.

A small item here regarding the different scaffold lifts for different trades: bricky, wanting his own way as always, will want to dictate the heights of the lifts without a second thought about the cost to you for adaptions by Scaffold Co. However, with a bit of consulting with Carpentry Co and Roofing Co, a plan can be hatched to save both effort and money.

Now any roofing chippy worth his salt should know what timbers and other materials are required in place to provide fixings for the roof covering, but it would be a good idea to have Roofing Co round before Carpentry Co proclaims that the roof is ready, just to make sure. A couple of missed timbers in the valley can lead to corners being cut by the roofer.

On the subject of H&S, as far as dangerous tools are concerned, obviously roofing chippy is using circular and sometimes bench saws, where the dangers speak for themselves; they should thus only be used by competent and confident tradesmen. However, there is one specific tool that should be mentioned: the nail gun.

Usually driven by gas (sometimes air) a nail gun fires a nail by exploding a gas, which shoots what is effectively a projectile into the timber. You do not need much imagination to consider the ramifications of abusing this tool. I have witnessed a few very near misses in the recent years when nail guns have been in common use, and I have also recorded a couple of accidents where it did not miss. What is underestimated often is that if the nail does not quite go where intended (hits a knot, for example) it will charge off on a different trajectory with sometimes disastrous results. It is very easy to become complacent using such a dangerous piece of kit, so as CDM policeman, be very mindful of someone using one.

Now, a paragraph on timber stress grading: whoever has designed the loose cut roof for building regs – more often the structural engineer – will have specified certain strength grades of timber to be used, especially for the rafters and so on. The timber would be stamped with a 'C' prefix such as C16 or C24, which relates to the strength, usually involving the number and size of knots, with the higher number denoting stronger timber. The grade has to be confirmed with the merchant when ordering, as it is entirely likely that the merchant would stock both, but the higher numbered timber would be more expensive, with obvious temptations. I will not go into the somewhat boring detail of how the timber is graded, but I will mention that it is extremely important that you use the correct grade and more importantly be aware that such a distinction exists.

Apart from the obvious need to use the correct timber for the job, all BC or BW inspectors have their pet interests, and it could be just your luck that yours picks up on the wrong timber used if you do not police accordingly, which could result in all manner of tears before bedtime.

A trussed roof is usually used for cost, but it can also be designed to eliminate additional steel support, as it is engineered entirely differently, and will sometimes support in ways that a cut roof cannot. It will also usually be supported on just the outside walls, providing flexibility with internal layouts. It will be designed by timber engineers at Truss Co, so timber grading and so on will be taken care of by them.

The main advantage of a trussed roof, however, is that of speed, since a great deal of the works have been undertaken in a factory, brought to site on a lorry, and then lifted with a crane. A drawing showing the different components and their exact place will have been issued by Truss Co, so this form of roof structure arguably requires a different level of competence and skill to construct on site.

A similar schedule of other trades takes place to construct gables and so on, but both types of roof structure will require all manner of bracing to give it its lateral strength and support.

On the subject of bracing, when your BC or BW inspectors come around to inspect at this stage (they will!), the things they are looking for is correct bracing, clips, straps, bolts, and so on, so pay strict attention to this with roofing chippy to avoid embarrassment.

Truss Co will provide the structural calculations and design required by BC, so make sure you lay your hands on them to pass on to BC.

Usually, in both cases (loose or trussed), a crane will be required – certainly with trusses – which again should be part of Carpentry Co's brief, along with any CDM requirements.

In most cases, part of roofing chippy's brief will be to fix fascia and soffit boards. If you are using a uPVC fascia, it is good practice to fix a timber- or ply-backing board to support both the fascia and later the guttering.

I know that we tend to not use timber fascia quite so much these days, but if you do, please make sure that the back is primed (painted) before it is fixed. This has nothing to do with protection, but in the case of solid timber, priming prevents it from cupping later if only one side is painted.

On the subject of treatment for roofing components:

Technically, as a rule of thumb, if an area is vented, then the roof components need not be treated to satisfy building regs. But if, say, in the case of a vaulted ceiling or warm roof area where not all of the timber component is vented, then the timbers must be treated – usually by pressure impregnation.

For this reason, most truss manufacturers will offer treatment as an extra over, since, if you think about it, simple trussed roofs with a flat ceiling are in a vented (roof)space.

Conversely, a lot of cut roofs are so designed to have rooms in the roof, and therefore, with a warm roof design. Thus, the timbers should be of the treated type. It is actually quite rare these days for timber merchants to stock carcassing-sized timbers that are not treated.

You may have gathered, dear reader, that when I was on the tools as a carpenter, my favourite aspect of the trade was roofing; so you may have picked up that I have a somewhat romantic view of the talents required for the job.

First fix

'First fix' and 'second fix' are terms used in several aspects of the construction industry, with first fix usually referring to work that is done before Plastering Co turns up. In the case of carpentry, this would include, for example, building the wall, studding, roof, ceiling, and any other noggins (timbers fixed into the structure for the fixing of other components), door linings/frames, window boards, and floor decking. The second fix is the finishing work, usually done after the plastering.

After completing the first fix, a carpenter would then stand back to allow other trades to work – for example, the electricians may lay cables or the plumbers may fix pipes in the roof, walls, and floor.

Regarding which chippy is likely to take this aspect, the subject is open to debate. Arguably, in the main, it involves a fair bit of carcassing work, but it also involves elements of the 'pretty side', such as door linings and window boards, which have to be cut and fixed carefully. Take the door linings for example. It seems like a straightforward enough job: they need to be fixed before plastering works, but they have to be fixed with precision to ensure that when, at second fix stage the door is swung, it will fit without drama. A second fix chippy hates following on behind door linings fitted by others for all sorts of reasons.

If you have several studwork walls, talk to the mechanical trades to see what noggins (timber support fixings) they may require before tacking (plasterboard fixing) takes place. The largest requirements come from plumbers, who need fixings for radiators and sanitary ware (including shower doors), so you need to have a pretty good idea where everything is eventually going, even at this early stage. The subject is more involved with timber frame than masonry, and don't forget fixings for kitchen cabinets.

On the H&S front, whist first fix carpentry inherently does not carry the same risks as, say, roofing, chippy is still working with power tools and sharp implements than can hurt badly if not used carefully, often the nail gun, which has been mentioned in the preceding section.

By this stage of the proceedings, we are all roofed in, with windows and so on in place and a scaffold outside, which will all dramatically affect the light levels, especially in the winter months. With this in mind, the temporary internal lighting should not be ignored, because accidents will happen in poor light.

Another H&S consideration is that it is most unlikely that the stairs will be fixed, so particular attention should be given to the stairwell and landing on the first floor, and even more so in case of a three-storey construction. We have a serious fall hazard here that can quite easily be addressed by temporary balustrades, platforms, and more.

Second fix and finishings

When plastering works are complete, the carpenters can then continue with the second fix work. This may be done by the same or a different carpenter as the first fix, and it would include fixing doors, architrave, window boards, stairs, and skirting – in other words, the works that will be on show and not covered up by plaster.

At this stage, chippy works very precisely with a van full of tools to suit, showing that, for example, a decently trained carpenter will know exactly how much gap to leave around the newly swung door or to leave a slight rattle when fixing the door stops, both to allow for several coats of paint without the need for further adjustment later.

As I mentioned earlier, the mind-set of the chippy conducting this stage of the works is different from the earlier stages. However, ironically, whilst arguably this is the element of the build that requires the highest level of skill, it seems to be the element most likely to be undertaken by the not so skilled or even DIYer with very simple tools and materials.

I suppose that is entirely likely that with the introduction of more and more power tools, the requirement for craftsmanship has somewhat diminished on your average build.

Showing your age there, Holden. You will be waffling on about how you used to sharpen your saw, chisels, and plane irons every Friday afternoon when you were a young chippy next!

The carpentry aspect of the second fix almost speaks for itself and does not really need much more from me, since there are so many permutations to what happens now according to individual requirements. From an H&S point of view, it is very similar to the first fix but with slightly different implements.

24

Roof Coverings

Roofing is split fundamentally into two areas: pitched and flat. A pitched roof is usually a slate or tile of numerous shapes and sizes; the flat roof is usually a felt, single ply, or GRP. In both cases, there are other materials involved, usually metals such as copper, zinc, or lead.

Roofers are definitely a breed of their own. I can say this with conviction, since for about 12 years in the late eighties and nineties, I had my own Roofing Co specialising in the application of large slating works such as churches, supermarkets, and office blocks. At the time, there was a huge preference for both natural and manmade slates. The domestic market was more steered towards tiles of different shapes and materials.

During this time, I took it upon myself to learn and understand the technicalities and obtain specialist knowledge in this field. This included, on one occasion, a trip to France so I could be instructed by a well-known slate quarry on the art of numerous slating techniques that Europe is well known for.

Back to the roofer. If you ever have contact with the flotsam and jetsam of the construction industry, it will be on the roof. Roof covering is a very labour-intensive trade; therefore, for every skilled tradesman, there are up to three others loading, fetching, and carrying. This results in the roofer sometimes enlisting the help of, shall we say, not the type you would want your daughter bringing round for Sunday Lunch with gran.

These labourers run a close second to the scaffolder in the wolf-whistling contingent, and in the theatre that is the construction site, due to their elevated position, they take centre stage. The roofer is probably the most likely to upset the natives.

The training for this trade is rarely formal, with the roofer's labourer promoted to roofer's mate and then on to roofer tradesman simply by being taught numerous aspects of the trade right there on the roof. It is more repetitive than skilful; many good roofers do not really understand the technicalities of what they are fixing. Therefore, it is quite an easy trade to learn to become proficient at a decent level. According to geography mainly, there are roofers who have never laid a tile and those who have never needed to master the techniques of slating.

Generally speaking, on site, they tend to keep themselves to themselves in terms of other trades, often because when they are plying their trade, they are the only ones on site at the time.

They are inherently very messy and carry certain H&S headaches for you.

- If ever someone is removing boards from the scaffold (to make a run up), it will be the roofer.

- If ever someone is taking out a handrail (to land materials) even though there is a loading bay just round the corner, it will be the roofer.

- If ever a trade leaves the scaffold knee high in waste, it will be the roofer.

- If you ever catch someone wearing footwear more suitable for the beach than a construction site, it will be a roofer.

- If you ever catch someone launching debris off the scaffold, it will be the roofer.

The main reason for these behaviours is the high turnaround of the unskilled labour, who can – if thrown off site for flagrant disregard for H&S or the sanity of neighbours – easily get another job and be replaced. So without doubt, you will have your work cut out with this trade.

Pitched Roof Coverings

There are many different types of roof tiles and slates made from various materials, which come in an assortment of shapes and sizes using a range of different colours and finishes.

To help get your head around the all these options, it is worth understanding a little about roof tile design. Most products available today have evolved from just three original types of roof covering that were first introduced hundreds of years ago, and that still remain popular today. They have been enlisted below:

- **Slate:** Thin rectangular sections of quarried metamorphic rock that come in varying sizes and thicknesses

- **Plain Tiles:** Small rectangular sections of clay with a smooth or sanded surface finish

- **Pantiles:** A distinctive clay or concrete tile with an 'S' shaped profile.

The principal designs outlined above have evolved over the last 70 years, with the new mainstream tiles and slates still falling into one of the aforementioned family of products.

Tile design developed with added features to improve performance and reduce cost first in the 1950s, when manufacturers began to use concrete to create more economical plain tiles and pantiles. In the '60s and '70s, after successfully copying clay tiles in concrete, manufacturers went one step further by taking the traditional pantile and roman tile designs and developing them into larger interlocking concrete tiles. These new designs were quicker, easier, and therefore cheaper to install. The same approach was applied to slate, which resulted in alternatives made from concrete and fibre cement. More recently, new clay tile designs that match concrete in size and ease of installation have appeared, in addition to composite materials that emulate natural slate. There are also new concrete tiles that take on a slate appearance, creating cost-effective natural alternatives to traditional slate. In short, all slate and tile coverings have several alternative materials.

One of the key constraints of roof tile design is the planning system, which often demands that new and refurbished roofs reflect traditional and local styles. This is one of the reasons that new tile designs do not stray too far from the original and traditional. Instead, manufacturers create hybrids that introduce added benefits but remain respectful towards each tile's origins.

Nowadays we are spoilt for choice. The renaissance in demand for traditional items made from materials such as slate and clay means there is now a greater choice of natural roofing materials than has been available for many years.

There has also been plenty of innovation driven by the need to minimise build costs with a growing demand for larger labour-saving designs. Many of these advanced materials are still made from clay and slate, but in Europe, providing more cost-effective options and availability to satisfy planning constraints. This can mean savings for many homeowners.

It also means that the aesthetic benefits of natural materials are now within most budget limits. One of the reasons clay tiles and slates remain popular today is that natural materials do not lose their colour. However, due to their manufacturing process, traditional materials have been beyond the reach of many budgets. Up until recently, those wanting their roof to keep its looks in the long term had to buy traditional materials such as clay plain tiles, pantiles, or natural slates. These products can range from double to even four times the cost of a large-format concrete tile roof. The arrival of more affordable modern made products means that you can build a clay roof for only a few hundred pounds more than concrete.

Slates and Slate Alternatives

The term slate can have two meanings: it can refer to the actual material, but it is also be used as a loose term to describe a type of roof material with a thin, flat appearance and (usually) a bluish/grey colour.

Natural slates are essentially thin sheets or slabs of metamorphic quarried rock that are laid double lapped, with each slate nailed to the batten or secured using special slate hooks. Slate has been used as a roofing material since Roman times, and it comes in many sizes, thicknesses, and levels of quality, which vary from region to region. The UK slate industry peaked in the 1980s, and today there are only two active quarries in Wales and small-scale specialist production in Devon and the Lake District. Most slate now tends to be imported and comes from countries such as Spain, China, Canada, and Brazil. Though most of the slate comes from abroad, slate from the UK has maintained a reputation for being of the highest quality and most durable. Welsh Slates from the Penrhyn, Ffestiniog, and Cwt-y-Bugail quarries remain popular, and they are known to be the finest roofing slates in the world, adorning many of our nation's finest buildings. Examples include Buckingham Palace, No 10 Downing Street, and St Pancras station.

Slate alternatives:
There are a number of alternatives to slate that have been developed to look similar and cost less. The most common alternatives are made from fibre-cement and concrete. Whilst these materials offer savings over the cost of slate, they struggle to compete with the aesthetics of natural quarried slate. Some interesting and more aesthetically pleasing alternatives exist in recycled slate and natural clay.

Thin leading edge clay and concrete tiles:
Thin leading edge tiles began as concrete and more recently became available in clay. The tiles come in slate colours and have been designed with a thin front edge to look more like slate. This thin leading edge is nearly half the thickness of standard flat concrete tiles, which are often rejected by planners for appearing too heavy on the roof.

This group of tiles come at a premium over standard concrete but still at half the cost of a slate roof due to the material and labour savings. Clay thin leading edge tiles are a recent innovation: they take advantage of the versatility of clay by providing a high-performance labour-saving slate alternative that, like slate, will not lose its colour over time.

Fibre-cement:
Fibre-cement was invented in the 1890s and uses layers of cellulose, which reinforces the fibres and cement. These slates have the same form and thickness as natural slate and offer value for money, but they cannot match slate's durability or longevity of colour.

Reconstituted/Recycled slate:
These products are made of crushed slate and other aggregates and are pressed with resins, sometimes in the format of an interlocking tile. Despite the fact that these products are tiles and not slate, because they are so thin, they still achieve an appearance close to that of natural slate. There are several products that are made in the shape of natural slates and are flat, thus giving a more realistic appearance. A big benefit of recycled slates is that they make use of the large amounts of waste material generated when quarrying slate, and they are offered by most leading manufacturers.

Asbestos Cement slates:
From the Second World War up to the 1960s, there were slates made with an element of Chrysotile asbestos (ACM's), which were most often square shaped and for some reason mainly laid in a diagonal pattern. This pattern will help you identify them if found on your roof today.
For obvious reasons they are no longer manufactured in the UK, and clearly, they carry all manner of implications if you have to remove them, and many challenges to match if you need to leave them on the roof and patch them up.

Plain Tiles

The plain tile is a small rectangular flat tile measuring 265 mm x 165 mm (or 10½" x 6½" x ½"). The size of plain tiles goes back hundreds of years and it does not vary much from that today.

Plain tiles are laid with a broken bond, and they keep out the water by overlapping each other three tiles deep. This results in only the bottom third of each tile being visible once laid. Tiles that are laid this way are known as double-lapped tiles, and they take their name and looks from this method of installation.

In addition to the standard tile, plain tiles require a 'tile and a half' or gable tile to be used down the verges (each side of the roof slope). They also require special 'eaves' tiles, used on the bottom course (row) of tiles.

Further, specially moulded tiles are required at the valleys and hips.

As a result of their small size and the fact that they do not interlock, plain tiles require around 60 tiles per square metre to be labour intensive to install. Also, there are up to three times more battens per square metre compared to interlocking tiles, and the weight on the roof is significantly greater.

There are a number of different tile types that vary in price and aesthetics:

Handmade clay plain tiles:

At the upper end of the price range are handmade clay plain tiles, where every tile has its own character, adding a rich texture to the roof, both in terms of colour and shape. Handmade plain tiles are normally lightly sanded, which further adds to their charm. As they are made of clay, the beauty of the roof will never fade; instead, it will mature slowly with age.

Handcrafted clay plain tiles:
The term handcrafted refers to machine-made plain tiles that have been carefully designed to have a handmade appearance, but at a more affordable price. Like the handmade variety, these tiles usually have a sanded texture and are available in similar colours. Over the years, the appearance of such tiles has improved, thanks to more sophisticated manufacturing techniques that achieve levels of character and texture, which closely resemble handmade plain tiles.

Clay plain tiles:
Machine-made clay plain tiles are available in a wide range of colours in the red/brown spectrum and all the way through to black. They usually have a smooth finish and are either double or single cambered. They generally cost 20% more than concrete plain tiles.

Concrete plain tiles:
Concrete plain tiles are the same size and shape as clay plain tiles and are available in colours that seek to mimic the appearance of clay plain tiles. The price of a concrete plain tile is generally slightly less than standard clay equivalents. Having said that, it is worth noting that the pigmented colour of concrete in these tiles will fade over time.

Interlocking plain tiles:
In an effort to reduce labour costs and use less material and energy, manufacturers now offer a number of interlocking hybrid plain tiles that require fewer tiles per square metre.

Clay interlocking plain tiles have proved particularly popular as they create a plain tile appearance for less than the price of a concrete plain tile. Such are the savings in material and labour, that these tiles reduce roof costs by around 40%. Interlocking plain tiles can also be laid at lower pitches than traditional plain tiles, which make them perfect for extensions and additions.

Pantiles

Original traditional pantiles are usually made from clay, and in cross section, they appear in a rather flattened 'S' shape. This shape creates a distinctive flowing appearance that over the years has given pantiles the reputation for being one of the UK's great vernacular roofing materials.

 Pantiles were originally made from clay until the 1950s, when more cost effective concrete pantiles appeared. The design of the concrete pantile is very similar to traditional clay pantiles; however, there are some aesthetic differences, which is why planners will not always permit the use of the concrete version. The concrete pantile has a thicker and rougher front edge of 30 mm (compared to 15 mm for a traditional clay pantile and around 20 mm for an interlocking pantile). The other key difference is colour: clay pantile colours have a more natural appearance, and as they are fired in a kiln, they will not fade over time like concrete products will.

Pantiles are generally found down the east coast of England and Scotland and in pockets around the southwest. This geographic spread began around the sixteenth century, when trading ships exported textiles to Holland and Belgium and returned to ports like Ipswich and Hull with clay pantiles.

As a result of the geographical nature of pantiles, not all roofers will know how to install them. If you are outside or on fringes of a pantile area, it is worth ensuring that you talk to a contractor who has experience laying such products.

Concrete pantiles have existed since the 1960s and have been popular due to labour- and time-saving benefits. The concrete double pantile is one of the most cost effective roof coverings available and hence a very popular roof tile shape in the UK.

Roman Tiles

The profile of the Roman tile design is a flat shape with a small roll running down the right hand side of the tile. Like pantiles, Roman style tiles are available in single and double form; however, unlike pantiles, the use of clay single Roman tiles is relatively limited.

It is more common to see double Roman roof tiles, particularly in concrete, with all major concrete manufacturers offering a concrete double Roman, which has held the position as the most popular roof tile for many years.

Roofing Underlays

Roofing felt was introduced primarily to act as a secondary barrier against wind-driven snow and rain. However, there is another little-known reason: to help avoid the positive and negative air pressure that can be caused within the roof space in exposed areas that can lead to tiles being 'drawn off' on the negative side.

Its use therefore can reduce the much needed air movement within the roof space, particularly if the roofing felt is impervious. This effect is often compounded by the introduction of insulation.

There are several forms of underlay commonly used in roof construction, the most popular until recent years being traditional bituminous felts, giving way to vapour permeable underlays and impermeable plastic products.

Vapour-permeable underlays, more commonly referred to as 'breathable' underlays, offer many advantages over the more traditional bituminous-based underlays and are rapidly becoming the first choice of designers, builders, and roofers. Breathable underlays let the building breathe by allowing the passage of water vapour outwards and so cut down, or in many cases, eliminate altogether, the need for roof space ventilation.

Impermeable plastic underlays can be used with adequate roof space ventilation and are particularly beneficial in situations where the roof tiles are being laid on a roof that is below the recommended minimum roof pitch by creating a waterproof sub-roof below the tiles.

Without getting too technical, the purpose of a breathable membrane is not only to allow the passage of air into the roof-space but also to permit the moisture-laden air out. The moisture passes out through the membrane, forms a dew point on the back of the tile or slate, and drips back down onto the membrane and runs off. For this reason, the membrane is 'one way' and has to be laid the correct way up with a certain distance from the underside of the tile formed by the tile batten and a sag of the membrane between the rafters.

Some BC and BW providers will accept a breathable membrane as sufficient to ventilate the roof space and some will not, insisting on additional ventilation methods in the form of fascia vents or slate/tile vents accompanied by a ventilating ridge system.

25

Plumbing

For the sake of this chapter, I will use the generic term Plumber for works on anything involving water.

The typical plumbing firm (could be a one-man band) that you are looking for tends to fall into two categories: the domestic plumber who would be involved in, say, changing your bathroom suite or kitchen taps, and the plumber who is more at home with larger projects, such as the major refurb or new build.

In my humble opinion, the first type is not at all suitable for the level of works that you are no doubt thinking of when reading this book, for numerous reasons that we will explore in a minute. The second type is also in turn often separated into what are in effect two separate trades: plumbing works and heating works. Again, we will explore this further in this chapter.

The one trait that they all share, however, is that they will pitch up to your job in a van the size of a removal lorry, rammed to the gunwales with just about every pipe, fitting, and tool known to man. They will then proceed to disgorge the entire contents of the aforementioned pantechnicon inside the house, even if only visiting site to fill up and test it. Make no mistake – when the plumbers are in town, there is no room for anyone else!

Plumbers are in the top three noisiest trades on the site, not in the same way as say the scaffolder with boisterous behaviour. No, plumbers just make a lot of noise – with tools, clanging pipes, and general communication. There would be no point in them having a radio – no one would hear it!

Plumbers need good manual dexterity. This includes the ability to hold the arm and hand steady when supporting a tool, piece of pipe, or cup of tea. Vision should be a keen attribute to allow the plumber to line up fittings properly, use a tape measure, and spot at a glance if a cheque is not signed. Occasionally, a plumber may need to work in a prone position or in cramped spaces, so the ability to do so while maintaining coordination between multiple limbs and dignity is important. Most people believe the term 'builder's bum' was invented for brickies. Wrong! It was for plumbers.

Like the sparky, they tend to come and go with borderline too much work on the go, so again, take with a pinch of salt the plumber's proposed programme.

Having said all of the above, finding the right plumber is equal to winning the lottery.
Plumber needs more than a decent level of knowledge of most things construction, since probably 90% of his work is hidden by the end of the job, so with this in mind and the fact that he is dealing with what is probably your worst enemy – water – finding a well-experienced conscientious plumber is paramount.

It's no wonder they earn almost as much as a dentist or A380 Airbus pilot: you are trusting them with your dream home. I do not need to tell you of the potential for tears, nervous breakdowns, or even divorce if water is to be found cascading down the dining room wall the day before the removal company arrive. The choice of plumber is probably the most important decision that you will make on the entire build, so choose wisely.

I am fortunate that I have had a long-standing (25 years or more) relationship with what I consider to be just about the best medium size plumbing firm that I have ever encountered. I used him for all of my works when I was a building contractor, and I recommend him as a first option to all of my clients nowadays. Most listen to me. Some do not! This plumber falls squarely in the middle with cost – not the cheapest but not the most expensive either. Value for money? Certainly! However, some Mr and Mrs SB are cost driven and do not always understand the relevance. I am sure that I need not spell it out any further. What he does provide, however, is a complete knowledge of plumbing and heating, in terms of both mechanics and technical knowledge, i.e. water board regulations. His airing cupboard pipework is worthy of a National Arts award (he even takes photos), and as a person would give you his last Rolo. Gold dust or rocking horse **** does not even come close, which is why I use him time after time – no headaches for me or my clients.

Qualifications

Any self-respecting plumber who claims to be in a professional position to work on your home will

- Have at least NVQ Level 3 with an organisation such as City & Guilds; and

- Be a member of a governing body such as Chartered Institute of Plumbing & Heating Engineering (CIPHE), the Association of Plumbing and Heating Contractors (APHC) and/or the Gas Safe Register (GasSafe) – formerly Council of Registered Gas Installers (CORGI).

Of these governing bodies;

- **CIPHE** is made up of individuals from a wide range of backgrounds, such as consultants, specifiers, designers, public health engineers, lecturers, trainers, trainees and practitioners, so it is aimed at larger companies, not one-man bands.

- **APHC** is a not-for-profit trade body for the plumbing and heating industry in England and Wales and represents large companies working on commercial projects, to sole traders working in domestic properties. This is the organisation that your average small Plumbing Co should be a member of since it sets standards, codes of practice, and technical support at this level.

- **GasSafe** is the official gas registration body for the United Kingdom appointed by the relevant health and safety authority for each area. By law, all gas engineers must be on the Gas Safe Register. (Gas Safe Register replaced CORGI as the gas registration body in Great Britain on 1 April 2010.)

On the H&S front, apart from the more obvious general issues covered elsewhere, the main specific H&S requirement is for gas. Anyone employed to work on gas appliances in domestic premises (that can involve gas fires and cookers) must be a Gas Safe registered engineer and competent in that area of gas

214

work. The gas engineer's competencies, and therefore areas he is qualified to work in, are clearly marked on the back of the engineer's Gas Safe Register ID card, which consumers are encouraged to ask an engineer for before they have gas work carried out in their home. The front of the card has a photograph, a registration number, and an expiry date, and the reverse shows the different categories of work that the engineer is qualified to undertake, for example, cookers, boilers, and gas fires. Do not assume that an engineer qualified to work on boilers can sign off on your gas fire.

Regulations apply to dictate what appliances can be used in which areas, such as gas heaters (even for water) in bedrooms. But again, your Gas Safe registered engineer would know all of this as part of his training. Under the Gas Safety (Installation and Use) Regulations 1998, for a gas engineering business to legally undertake gas work that is within the scope of the regulations, they must be on the Gas Safe Register.

These rules also apply to carbon monoxide (CO), its existence, and its preventative measures. CO is a colourless and odourless gas, making its presence difficult to detect. It is formed when domestic fuels such as gas, coal, wood, and charcoal are burnt. When fuel burns in an enclosed room, the oxygen in the room is gradually used up and replaced with carbon dioxide. If carbon dioxide builds up in the air, the fuel is prevented from burning fully and starts releasing carbon monoxide instead.

There are several building regulations that also apply in this regard. Part L of the Building Regulations is concerned with the conservation of fuel and power in buildings. Regulations also bear on the energy performance of dwellings and their heating systems.

For new dwellings, the provision of heating and hot water services systems has to be considered as part of the overall design of the building. For works on heating and hot water services systems in existing dwellings, the provision is determined by such things as BR requirements including Standard Assessment Procedure (SAP) calculation.

Putting aside the numerous calculations of the proposed system that affect aspects such as the SAP calculation (see below), the documentation required for Building Regulations that affect new heating systems in new or existing dwellings generally falls under the Benchmark system. This is a boiler commission checklist that is completed by the approved installer (usually also Gas Safe registered – see below) and proves compliance with the relevant building regulations. Most boiler manufacturers include the Benchmark checklist at the back of the installation manual, which also provides part of the warranty registration for the boiler. Building control would usually want sight or copy of this completed document, but the hard copy would stay with the owner.

If you have a new gas appliance fitted, your Gas Safe registered engineer must let your local authority know. This is achieved through a self-certification process known as notification. Registered engineers have the duty to comply with Building Regulations by installing gas appliances and then notifying the appliance to the relevant LA. However, that duty is also shared to an extent with the property owner, as the responsibility ultimately falls upon the property owner to ensure that Building Regulations are complied with. Further, the property owner may be the focus of any Building Regulations related enforcement action by the LA if the work is not notified. Once your engineer notifies they have fitted a new heat-producing gas appliance in your home, you will receive a Building Regulations Compliance Certificate.

It is important to keep both the Benchmark document and this certificate safe, as they may be needed if you sell your home or if you choose to re-mortgage. These documents belong with the property, so if you sell your home, then they will need to be passed on to the next owner.

Plumbing Works

Plumbing works hinge mainly around the provision of hot and cold water to the numerous stations such as bathrooms and kitchens.

Hot water systems provide hot water around the home and are relatively straightforward, with the majority of new homes having an unvented hot water system or direct hot water system fed from a combination boiler.

Currently, there are three main types of hot water systems in use in the UK: open vented, unvented, and instantaneous.

Open vented hot water systems:
This system uses many different parts to heat water. It consists of a hot water cylinder, a cold water storage cistern (tank), special pipework (known as an open vent pipe), and a heat source to heat the water. There are two types of open vented hot water: direct heating and indirect heating.

- Direct heating: The water is heated directly from the heat source either by an immersion heater or by the boiler

- Indirect heating: The central heating and the hot water are separate; the water is heated via a coil (heat exchanger) from a boiler

Unvented hot water systems:
These systems are far more complicated, but do allow near mains pressure hot water supply. They are designed to still have a hot water storage tank such as a Megaflow; they do away with the cold water storage tank; and they operate at a much higher pressure than the open vented system.

Instantaneous hot water heating systems:
This method involves using gas or electricity to heat the water to a useable temperature without the need to store the water. The electric versions use a coiled heating element to heat the water rapidly in a manner similar to a kettle or immersion heater.

The most common method to heat water is the use of a combination boiler. This type of boiler works by using the circuit that powers the central heating and diverting it to another 'water to water' heat exchanger (heat swapping). This part swaps out the heat from the heating water to the hot water parts of your home.

Heating Works

Central heating systems within a domestic property are often overlooked and taken for granted. Understanding the components of a central heating system and how it all works will help occupants of a property manage its maintenance requirements and seek help and advice when needed.

Boiler:
The boiler is the main component of a central heating system. They come in several sizes, delivering various amounts of heat energy, fuel types, and energy ratings.

Size:

The amount of heat energy (measured in kilowatts or kW) a boiler is required to deliver through the home is based on a series of calculations carried out by an experienced and qualified plumber. They will be determined by the size of property, the building construction, building materials, and how the boiler will be used.

Type of fuel:

There is a wide range of boilers that burn a range of fuel types. Below is a list of the most common types:

- Natural gas: Burns methane from the gas mains in most towns and cities

- LPG: Burns liquid petroleum gas, normally propane or butane

- Oil type C2: Burns kerosene, which is the same as jet fuel

- Oil type D: Burns 'gas oil' used mainly in oil Agas

- Solid mineral fuel: Burns coal or coke

- Biomass fuel: Burns wood logs, pellets or chippings

- Electric: Works like a kitchen kettle but on a much bigger scale

SAP rating

This is the seasonal efficiency performance or the energy efficiency rating of a boiler and is listed in terms of Bands A to G. Band A is the best rating with at least 90% efficiency and Band G is the worst with only 70% efficiency or below. SAP 2009 energy-efficiency bands are as follows:

- Band A: 90% and above
- Band B: 86%–90%
- Band C: 82%–86%
- Band D: 78%–82%
- Band E: 74%–78%
- Band F: 70%–74%
- Band G: Below 70%

Building Regulations ensure that only the highest possible energy-efficiency boilers are fitted and prevent low-efficiency boilers from being fitted.

Types of boilers:

- Conventional boiler: This boiler is the most basic type. It just burns fuel to generate heat for central heating or hot water.

- System boiler: This boiler provides central heating only or heating and a store of hot water in a hot water cylinder (tank).

- Condensing boiler: This boiler uses the heat in the gases generated when the fuel is burnt; this reuse of normally wasted heat makes some of the steam in the waste gases condense into water, giving this boiler its name.

- Combination boiler: This boiler provides central heating and instant hot water.

Biomass boilers:
Technically, a wood-burning stove is biomass; link it to a back boiler and you have a biomass boiler.

Biomass boilers tend to be larger than their gas or oil equivalents. They are generally more suitable for people not connected to mains gas and who have some space for storage. You will need a reasonable area near where the boiler is sited to store the fuel, which is usually in the form of pellets.

Ideally, the fuel storage area will be under cover, as it is important to keep fuel dry. A higher moisture content in the fuel will reduce the efficiency with which it burns. If wood pellets get wet, they turn to unusable mush. This area also needs to be accessible for a delivery lorry. Wood pellets can be delivered loose and blown into a hopper, or in bags on a pallet.

The boiler will need a flue in which the vent material is designed for wood fuel (existing chimneys can be lined). The installation must comply with all relevant building regulations. If you live in a listed building or a conservation area, you will need to check with your local planning authority before fitting a new flue.

If fitting retrospectively, it is important to check whether the boiler will work with your existing plumbing, or whether it needs to be altered. Also find out how easy it will be to get the boiler serviced regularly and whether there are local plumbers or engineers who know how to work with it.

Next, find out if there is at least one, or preferably a choice of, local fuel suppliers, as the cost of fuel varies according to the distance the supplier has to travel. Not all suppliers offer all types of fuel. The lowest maintenance is in a tanker to a hopper. A pallet full of bags will involve more work feeding the boiler. Wood pellet boilers will need annual servicing.

Renewables

Then we have renewable technologies such as heat pumps. Put simply, a heat pump takes the available heat from the ground or air surrounding a property and increases it to a more useful temperature for use in the home. This renewable source of heat can be used to create warm air or water (for space and central heating) as well as hot water (for both central heating and domestic hot water supply).

It achieves this by taking the same principle that allows a fridge to cool your groceries and by utilising it in reverse. While air conditioners and freezers are familiar examples of heat pumps, the term 'heat pump' is more general and applies to many heating, ventilating, and air conditioning devices used for space heating or space cooling. When a heat pump is used for heating, it employs the same basic refrigeration-type cycle used by an air conditioner or a refrigerator, but in the opposite direction, releasing heat into the conditioned space rather than the surrounding environment. In this use, heat pumps generally draw heat from the cooler external air or from the ground. In heating mode, heat pumps are three to four times more efficient in their use of electric power than most other heaters.

Heating emitters: Radiators

The radiator is the most common way of heating your home. A radiator works by transferring heat to the air in the room as it passes over the radiator panel. Warm air rises and pushes colder air back down and over the radiator surface again. There are several types of radiators: many are made from copper or aluminium, but most are made from steel.

Heating emitters: Underfloor heating

Underfloor heating is a set of plastic pipes that are often run under a solid concrete floor surface, and which use the floor itself to heat the room by radiating heat upwards. This type of heating will generally only be fitted during a new build or extension or conservatory added to an existing property.

Consideration will have to be given to the floor covering. While tiles and wooden floors are ideal, deep pile carpets may have an adverse effect on the heating performance, acting as an insulator.

Plumbing Pipes

Plumbing pipes fall into two major categories, metal and plastic, but there are many different types in each category. Each type offers benefits and drawbacks, and some types of piping are more common than others are.

The two main popular materials now used are as follows.

Copper:

This type of pipe has been used since the early 1960s and is very reliable but expensive. Copper pipes are highly resistant to corrosion, tolerant of heat, and not prone to leaks, since the connections are soldered and fittings stay tight.
Copper pipes offer significant advantages. They are flexible, durable, and stable.

They last long and have a proven performance track record. They can be used indoors and outside. As they are . impermeable, they protect water from external contaminants and create a natural biostatic environment that resists bacterial growth inside. These pipes resist corrosion better than other metal piping and have an estimated lifespan of 50-70 years. Copper's reputation for reliability adds value to homes at resale, because homebuyers consider it a desirable feature. Copper piping can be safer than other piping methods because it resists burning and doesn't release toxic gases in a fire.

The downsides are few but important. Copper piping can freeze and snap in extreme cold. Acidic water can cause corrosion and leach copper from the pipe, imparting a metallic taste and increasing copper levels in drinking water. Finally, copper piping's biggest drawback is the high fluctuating price, which is why copper is gradually being replaced by more economical plastic pipe types.

Cross Linked Polyethylene (PEX):

This type of pipe is used extensively for interior plumbing in new homes. PEX resists heat much better than most plastic pipes, so it is often used for water-based heating systems. Plumbers like it because it's durable, reliable, and flexible. It resists bursting, is comparatively easy to install, and requires fewer joints. Further, both initial connections and repairs are easier to make. Homeowners like it because these same factors increase confidence, eliminate hassles, and reduce costs. PEX has its shortcomings. It resists cold but degrades under UV light, so it is not used outdoors. The tubing can be permeated by outside contaminants, and the Association of Plumbing & Heating Contractors (ASTM) has assigned it an expected service life of just 25 years.

While up to 85% of existing homes have copper piping, many new homes are plumbed with PEX. To determine which is better for you, talk with your plumber. Instead of an either/or approach, many experienced plumbers will base recommendations on the specifics involved, such as suggesting copper for chlorinated water supplied by utilities and PEX for well systems and areas with acidic water.

So on to the actual works, as per with other trades, there is a first and second fix procedure for plumbing works as well. The first fix includes everything that is involved in the first stage of your build. First-fix plumbing is basically involves laying pipework for the water supply, space heating, and the wastewater drainage from your property. Second-fix plumbing is the process of actually connecting the appliances – this would also include testing and commissioning. Second-fix plumbing would include bathroom sanitary ware and radiators as well as boilers and other equipment.

First fix is mainly just installing pipes and internal drainage. Clearly, you will need to have agreed upon the positions of sanitary ware and kitchen layout, amongst other things, because as I mentioned earlier, the majority of these pipes are going to be covered up in one way or another.

A few little tips;

Since a lot of plumber's pipework, including waste and soil pipes, will be passing through floors, modern engineered joists are handy for many reasons, including no notching of joists or drilling holes.

If, as in the case with many refurb situations, the timber joists need to be notched or drilled, there are specific parameters that must be adhered to. The diagram below shows rules that need to be conformed to for Building Regulations and Warranty but should be included as good practice no matter what.

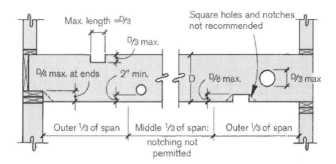

I-Joists have their own limitations set out by the individual manufacturer, and of course, metal web joists do not need any holes.

If plumber needs to notch or drill timber joists, make sure he places some form of cushioning between the pipe and timber. Briefly, copper pipes expand and contract; therefore, they rub on the timber if directly in contact, and become the perfect alarm clock when the heating kicks in first thing in winter months. This is another good reason to use plastic pipes, since they do not expand in the same way.

One way to tell a good plumber from a not-so-good plumber is the number of individual pipe circuits on the hot and cold water system. A good rule of thumb is to have as many of the items of sanitary ware individually piped back to the cylinder/main, especially showers. This to a very large extent saves you from scalding when enjoying your shower and someone flushes a toilet. Beware the plumber that wants to link them all together on one feed!

Never bury pipes in external block walls. Apart from the obvious screw through a pipe when hanging Mrs Self-build's favourite mirror, you are (subject to how deep you chop) potentially weakening the blockwork (cracks later) and providing a cold bridge from the cavity into the pipes and the room itself.

Make sure that any pipes in potentially thermal exposed positions – and this can sometimes mean in floors – are lagged with insulating material.

At the second fix or finishing stage, plumber effectively makes it all work (without leaks), and like most other trades, if he has done the first fix correctly, this stage should be straightforward.

A few pet hates of mine;

Never let plumber bury your shower tray or bath into the wall, especially if against plasterboard on studwork. The shower tray or bath should be effectively 'glued' to the wall with high modulus silicone, allowing the tiles to dress down onto the silicone, and then be sealed again between tiles and sanitary ware.

When fitting the shower doors, silicone should be applied on the outside. This application allows any water that gets between the components of the door assembly to drain inside and into the tray. I would love a pound for every time I have seen exactly the opposite, which means that any water that gets inside the frame (and it will) runs out and onto the floor.

I could go on and on about plumbing and almost fill a book in its own right, but suffice to say, if you have chosen well, he should know all of the above in any case.

On the heating front, there are entirely different programme logistics for a wet system with underfloor (u/f) heating and for that with radiators. With radiators, the pipework goes in at first-fix stage. With u/f heating, as a rule, the pipework goes in after plastering and just before floor screed or overboard. In both cases, the system should be filled and tested under pressure, with u/f being tested preferably until after screed is laid.

A significant difference between a radiator system and u/f is the amount of time it takes for the house to heat up and likewise cool down again, and so requires a different approach to the heating requirements. You cannot just 'pop the heating on' to take the chill off with u/f like you can with radiators.

U/f with a heat pump works at a much lower temperature (the temp of the water flowing through the pipes – not to be confused with the room temperature) than with a boiler, so again, the time taken to heat a space is different. With a heat pump, you would expect to switch the heating on in autumn and run it continuously through to spring.

Underfloor heating systems can be mixed with conventional radiator systems, but several issues must be considered. Note that the u/f heating system needs to be a complete separate system , i.e. the flow and return for underfloor heating needs to go all the way back to the boiler. If you do have radiators in your system, independent control from the boiler is required, i.e. not together with the underfloor heating.

There are all manners of insulation requirements that are far too numerous to go into here, but in most cases, over a concrete or block and beam floor for example, the insulation boards would provide the fixings for the u/f pipework until the screed or overboard are laid.

U/f heating pipes run back in individual room loops to a manifold, which in turn is fed from the boiler. This manifold holds the individual valves and controllers (actuators) which are controlled from the appropriate room stats.

With a radiator system, in majority of cases, the heat requirement is controlled by a room stat positioned to control the entire floor level. In larger properties, the areas would be zoned by floor (ground floor, first floor, and so on). These stats control motorised valves, which are usually positioned near the boiler.

Clearly, the information in this chapter offers only a brief overview, but it will hopefully arm you with fundamental knowledge and even make you sound like you know what you are talking about when choosing the right contractor.

Vince Holden

26

Electricians

Electricians are a funny lot, and they would rarely be found in the top three loud and boisterous trades on the site. They are usually fairly quiet and studious; their job being not so much physical but more technical, since they are dealing with what could be a life-threatening element that should never be underestimated – electricity!

Whilst sparky is not necessarily gregarious like, say, a scaffolder, he needs to be intelligent and up to speed with construction matters that affect his work. His radio will be tuned in to Radio 4 with the volume down, and his packed lunch will have either sandwiches with the crusts cut off or pasta in a little tub. They are not part of the arse hanging out your tracksuit brigade, and I have on occasion seen one wearing a tie.

I have known some right joker electricians – they just do it quietly.

Watch out for the sparky with the thousand-yard stare, a short attention span, and his hair standing on end. Despite what the Victorians thought of an electric shock being good for the heart, a sparky who has had too many belts displays a tendency to be either no good at his job or not focused enough to do it. Either way, he is not the one to be trusted to connect the spaghetti junction inside the consumer unit of your dream home.

A half-decent domestic sparky will have undertaken a four-year apprenticeship with NVQ or City & Guilds Level 3 and will have proved, amongst other things, his knowledge of technical working, health and safety, and building regulations in at least Part P.

Electricians always have more work on the go than the time to do it. A one-off domestic project such as your dream home will not fill out Sparky Co's order book for long, so he needs many jobs on the go at any one time. He will probably take a day or three to first fix an average new build with a similar time to second fix it. Factor in that works are rarely ready for him at a time originally planned, and you can see that he will have many plates spinning. With this in mind, don't be surprised if sparky comes and goes a bit, so build in a time buffer when programming his works in.

The H&S considerations are mainly obvious and the governing body that he should be a member of (I will get to that in a minute) will carry very stringent rules and codes of practice of its own. However, you as Client, Principal Designer, Project Manager, Site Manager, or a combination of all will need to keep your wits about you.

Here is a small excerpt from the Health and Safety Executive document, *Electricity at Work:*
Safe Working Practices:

21 - If you have managerial or supervisory responsibilities, it is important that you ensure that everyone knows how to work safely and without risk to their health, and that all workers follow the safety rules and control measures identified in risk assessments:

- you should be involved in planning the work and in the risk assessment process, coordinating the work where more than one group is involved, and discussing the necessary precautions and emergency procedures with the workers;

- you must clearly define the roles and responsibilities of the supervisors and workers, including those of any contractors who may be employed;

- you must ensure that supervisors are competent to supervise the work, with the level of supervision being appropriate to the danger and the competence of those carrying out the work;

- you must identify those people who are competent and have knowledge and experience of the electrical system to be worked on. Anyone who does not have this will need a greater level of supervision, or will need to be given adequate training to make sure that they have the correct skills, knowledge and risk awareness for the task. Do not let unauthorised, unqualified, or untrained people work on electrical systems.

Clearly, only some or all of the above will apply to you according to the works, but it's not a bad idea to have the regulations in mind, no matter what the scale. Just bear in mind also on this subject, that from an H&S point of view, it is not only about sparky himself that you have to consider; it's everyone on site!

There are two main governing bodies for domestic sparkies: Electrical Contractors Association (ELACSA) and National Inspection Council for Electrical Installation Contracting (NICEIC).

Sparky will need to be a member of at least one of these in order to officially sign off, and more importantly, certify his works for Building Regulations.

On all new build and a large portion of refurbs, BC will want to see a Part P certificate issued by Sparky Co. These days, sparky will complete the certification online, print off a copy, and give it to you, a copy of which you will then pass on to BC. The circuit is complete (pardon the pun) when the governing body makes their end public to BC. Your diligent BC surveyor will check this with them to make sure that the certificate (and more importantly the sparky) is authentic and so ticks the box.

It is a worthwhile small exercise then to confirm with Sparky Co before you accept his quote that he is a member of a recognised governing body and can come up with the goods at certificate time.

There are some electrical works on refurb and extension that do not require a Part P certificate but only a test certificate. A test certificate is just that, showing all the circuits (that sparky has worked on) with the test results. A Part P certificate is the test results plus more, concluding with an actual Building Regulations certificate.

Whilst a test certificate is only for you to prove that his works are tested, several factors decided whether or not it falls under Part P. This tends to hinge around the age and state of the consumer unit, but is not confined to this. A competent Sparky Co will advise on the whys and wherefores.

Whichever is prudent to your works, this paperwork is important, so keep it in a safe place for when you either sell or let the property.

So, on to the actual installation:

I can never emphasise enough the importance of working out your electrical layout at early doors. Discuss with sparky himself such things as switch positions and whether or not lights need to be two way (same lights switched at more than one place). Imagine where the furniture might go, where 'telly corner' will be, and so on. Once wired and plastered, it is not a small job to be moving such positions later, which can incur costs.

Don't expect architect or sparky to be a mind reader. This is a very personal aspect of the build requiring deep thought from you, since you will be the one living with it. Do not underestimate its importance – whilst professionals and tradesmen can give their two-penneth, it's down to your choices. So give it lots of thought.

All sparky wants to do when he pitches up is to get on with the job and not be spending hours with Mr and Mrs SB while they wander about the site waving arms about, generally arguing with one another and stroking chins.

I realise that quite a lot of you reading this find it difficult to imagine rooms until you can see them in the flesh. Just don't leave the job until the day sparky is due to address it.

Sparky can be one of the major players when it comes down to interrupting the integrity of the airtightness. In masonry, he might want to take a shortcut into or across the cavity, so watch him like a hawk. Any cables and other items that need to go from inside to outside need to be sleeved and sealed as they find their way through. Think of your first airtightness line of defence as the inside of the blockwork, and the cavity an uninterrupted passage for the leak. The same goes for with top floor ceiling board and lights, which recess into the roof void such as downlighters.

Subject to how serious you are taking the airtightness issue, there are numerous products and fittings that cater to these considerations. In the timber frame as well, the membrane on the inside is where you consider all punctures.

Your average sparky is not entirely familiar with this aspect since to the best of my knowledge, airtightness issues are not yet discussed in any detail at sparky school. It will therefore be your responsibility to police this issue, so re-read my previous chapter on the subject and get vigilant.

If you have chosen a decent tradesman and talked to death about your requirements, to be fair, apart from all the above, he should just get on with the job.

In masonry work, he has little choice but to completely first fix his cables into the back boxes that will be chopped into the blocks.

In timber frame or studwork, there are two ways of going about it. One is to fix back boxes onto timber noggins (support battens), which means the tacker has to be good with his measuring and cutting to guarantee a snug fit of the board around the box. This snug fit is important for a variety of reasons, including possible airtightness leaks. However, this also means that a large gap around the box will need filling with plaster or filler, and if the filled gap is larger than the actual front plate, there is a good chance of it falling out later when everything dries and shrinks a taste.

The second way is to let the tacker board over all the cables that are left loose in the studworks; then, sparky (having kept a careful note of where they all are) cuts a surface-mounted box into the plasterboard afterwards. This has a couple of benefits.

The plasterwork on the wall is completely smooth and not protruding slightly where the spread (plasterer) has skimmed across and around the back box aperture. Also, the box itself, which is usually plastic, will be a snug fit in a hole cut accurately by sparky himself. Such plasterboard boxes clamp themselves to the plasterboard and so do not require a noggin in the timberwork.

On the same subject, it is not uncommon, when using downlighters, for sparky to request that the tacker plasterboards over the entire ceiling in question and push the downlight cables up above. Once tacked and skimmed, sparky then cuts the hole for the downlighters, which again keeps the ceiling smooth. It is very difficult for the spread to keep the ceiling smooth as a pond if there are a dozen cables sticking out.

Having said all at this, the theory is only as good as sparky's map, which he would need to have drawn with the precise location of the downlighters.

Again, on the subject of downlighters, which some people want to pepper their ceilings with, there are a couple of considerations.

One is of airtightness, especially in upstairs ceilings, and the other is them overheating by coming into contact with insulation, which, let's face it, is most of the time (even in ceilings below a floor, there should be some form of insulation for sound). Numerous downlight fittings address both these problems, but obviously come at a cost, so do your homework.

So, Sparky is conducting his first fix, which mainly involves dropping cables down all over the place. Not much to say on that really, other than the fact that the cable drops should be capped or in conduits and always drop down vertically from the box, so you always have a good idea where the live cables are much later on when Mr SB gets his cordless out to hang your favourite picture.

A pet subject of mine here is that all sockets, switches, and so on should be set nice and level with one another. A half decent sparky will have a laser level set up for this exercise, and so will have no excuse but for them all looking to attention at the same level when Mrs SB's striped wallpaper or shelves goes up.

Likewise, at second-fix stage, you have no idea how many electricians seem to lose their balance when fixing the faceplates. It is not at all uncommon to see sparky with his boat level out when fitting the sockets – this is the sign of a good tradesman. Just watch out for a follow-on trade such as the decorator, who might want to loosen the front plates to paint his first coat behind but not employ the same millimetre-perfect eye when screwing them back on again, thus painting round them on the skew.

One last point I will make mainly regarding sparky's brief. There always seems to be a grey area of responsibility when it comes to boiler/heating controls and the plumber. Sometimes plumber will feel he should be twisting his own wires together, but that does not work well at sign off time, because more often than not, plumber will be providing the hardware (thermostats, programmer, and so on), as part of his kit. The best way forward is for plumber to supply the parts and for sparky to make it all work.

27

Mechanical Ventilation & Heat Recovery (MVHR)

There are several reasons why you would want to install an MVHR system in your home. Whilst with a new build, the advantages are easy to define, with refurb or renovation, it becomes more a style choice than a necessity.

With a new build, the most important aspect is compliance with Part F of Building Regulations, namely F1: means of ventilation. Without adequate ventilation, contaminants such as ammonia, acetic acid, methane, nitrogen monoxide, VOCs from paints and formaldehyde from cleaning products, not to mention the dust, odours, CO_2, and water vapour we produce each day, all linger in our homes and affect the health of our families. Indeed, the need for controlled ventilation is so important that Part F is largely devoted to the issue, which states the following:

- All fixed mechanical ventilation systems, where they can be tested and adjusted, shall be commissioned and a commissioning notice must be given to the Building Control Body within 5 days of completion.

- For mechanical ventilation systems installed in new dwellings, air flow rates shall be measured on site and a notice given to the Building Control Body. This shall apply to intermittently-used extract fans and cooker hoods, as well as continuously running systems.

- Ventilation provisions have been increased for dwellings with a design air permeability tighter than or equal to 5 m3/(h.m2) at 50 Pa.

What this effectively means is that if you are constructing a new build to any decent level of thermal performance with an airtightness reading of 5 or less (easily achieved), MVHR is almost obligatory and should be installed and commissioned by a competent person, with the test certificate provided to Building Control.

We used to be able to rely on local extractor fans in kitchen and bathrooms with trickle events in the windows to provide 'background ventilation', but that was before we became wise to the benefits of sealing up and insulating the build.

It is important for your property to breathe, especially when it is super-insulated and airtight for maximum energy efficiency. But if 'breathing' means removing warm air to replace it with cold air just to remove moisture, dust, and odours, there has to be a better more efficient way to ventilate a building.

How MVHR Works

Typically, 20%-30% of your space heating energy is lost through 'natural' ventilation: trickle vents in windows, extractor fans in wet rooms, open doors or other gaps in the building fabric. By sealing up the leaks and making your property more airtight, the flow of air can be more effectively controlled.

Improving airtightness only to then ventilate the property by opening windows is nonsense. Why rely on natural ventilation when heat recovery ventilation can swap stale air for fresh air without wasting energy?

The mechanical ventilation system uses super-efficient fans to feed fresh filtered air into living/work/sleep areas, at the same time pulling stale moist air from kitchens, bathrooms, and other indoor wet areas. The pressure differential gently controls the direction of the flow to provide fresh air where you need it, and create a balance accordingly.

The heat exchanger within the MVHR then recovers up to 90% of the warmth from the stale air before it leaves the building, transferring it from the old air to the new. You get fresh filtered air throughout your home without the excessive heat loss associated with traditional extract ventilation.

In a well-insulated building, a heat exchanger transfers up to 90% of the energy from the old air to the new, reducing overall space heating bills while at the same time improving air quality. Further savings are enabled by eliminating the need to open window casements, extractor fans, and trickle vents. Dry air also costs a lot less to heat than damp air.

Normally consuming less electricity than a light bulb, an MVHR system creates an always-on low-pressure air movement throughout the whole property. An MVHR system should pay for itself through energy-savings in around 5 years and have a working life in excess of 10 if not 20 years. Of all the energy-saving products on the market, MVHRs are generally believed to offer the greatest return on investment.

They are good for your health, your wallet, and the environment

However, it is not just simply about buying a box of tricks and a pile of ducting and then installing it. Let's face it; the actual mechanics of fixing ducting in place are not difficult, are they? The system has to be carefully designed to ensure that airflow rates are achieved and balance with the correct unit being chosen for its capability to ensure the air changes are achievable even at peak times.

Bearing in mind that most if not all of the ducting will be eventually hidden, it must be installed correctly. Most of the system and therefore its efficiency hinges around the ducting.

One key measure is the need for the ducting located in a cold area (for example, loft space) to be insulated. The insulation needs to be equivalent to 25 mm of thickness and have a thermal conductivity of 0.04 W/(m.k) or less. This ensures that condensation doesn't form due to the difference in air temperature inside the duct when compared to the air temperature in the cold space. If you don't have a loft space, there is still a need for insulated ducting on the intake and exhaust legs, as they will be carrying cold air in a warm space. The level of insulation can be achieved by wrapping PVC duct in a layer of rockwool for example, or by using a one-piece, insulated duct.

Size of Duct

The two most common duct sizes used are 125 mm diameter for circular and 204 mm x 60 mm for rectangular ducts. You may choose between these two sizes to suit your build, whether you have a shallow service void where the rectangular duct would be best, or if you're constructing using webbed joists where the circular duct may be most suitable. However, it is also important to remember that if you have a large volume of air being distributed around your home, a larger size duct may be utilised to keep in-duct air velocities as low as possible. This helps keeps the pressure resistance lower and your MVHR unit running more quietly.

Steer clear of flexible ducts

Building regulations will only allow a maximum length of 300 mm of flexible ducting to be used to overcome obstacles such as ceiling timbers. Although it may seem like a quick and easy way of running the ducting throughout your build, there are many drawbacks, not least its non-compliance. Flexible ducting will increase the resistive pressure applied to your MVHR unit when compared with a rigid duct. This in turn can have a negative effect on the unit's performance by increasing the fan speed and noise, whilst lowering its heat recovery efficiency.

Branched or Radial Ducting

A branched ducting system would have a main duct leg with T-pieces located along its length to branch off to each room that requires ventilation. This is a widely used method of supplying and extracting the air around a house. You can incorporate different sizes of ducting in the system as well as have silencers installed where desired.

A radial ducting system would involve having two manifold boxes connected back to the MVHR unit, one for extract and one for supply. From these manifolds, a semi-rigid length of 75 mm circular duct is extended to each room to provide adequate ventilation.

This method is becoming more popular, as it allows a certain amount of flexibility when it comes to the installation stage.

Where to Put the Unit

You must ensure that the location of the MVHR unit provides sufficient space to both undertake regular maintenance, such as filter changes, and allow for the unit in its entirety or key mechanical electrical components to be replaced without the need to remove fixed structures or ductwork.

You will need to provide a condense pipe similar to that required by a modern gas boiler, connected to a waste pipe on the drainage system, so bear this in mind when deciding where to site the unit. Placing it in a cupboard right in the middle of the house will require prior design for drainage in the same way as, say, a bath or washing machine.

A half decent MVHR unit will not make any noise or vibration, but consideration still needs to be used if say mounting the unit directly on the ceiling in the roof above the main bedroom and you are a light sleeper. There are numerous ways of isolating the unit for acoustics and vibration that do not require much imagination.

The unit will also require a dedicated fused spur, so sparky needs to have sorted this.

One thing that must be borne in mind is that MVHR – especially the unit itself – presents, quite ironically, an airtightness challenge, since inherently the unit is often within the airtightness fabric or layer, with the ducting often traveling in and out of the zone. There is no simple rule of thumb with this, but you will need to keep your wits about you when making decisions especially where to position the unit.

Quite often, it would be tempting to site the unit in a cupboard, but then the ducts that usually leave from the top will more than likely travel from an airtight environment up into floor or roof voids, which are not airtight. I try as much as possible to site the unit in the roof space for this reason.

On the subject of controls:

Generally speaking, once commissioned, your average MVHR unit just gets on with its knitting in the background. A decent one will incorporate an automatic boost and humidistat that senses when, say, the shower has been running and creating steam and thus requires a temporary surge. It would still have a manual override panel, which, provided the wiring has been installed at first fix, can be positioned wherever you want. You would very rarely need to use it if everything is working correctly, so this panel can be tucked away in a cupboard somewhere.

The only other built-in control that sorts the men from the boys is a summer bypass, which again should be automatic. It probably speaks for itself, but in summer months, you do not want your incoming fresh air passing over a heat exchanger that has removed heat from the outgoing moist air.

MVHR installation involves three visits from the engineer:

- First fix to install all the ducting

- Second fix to fix the unit and ceiling diffusers

- Commission, where all balancing and test certification info is created

Watch out for what MVHR Co will expect you, and not them, to do, such as cutting holes, installing external vent grilles, and connecting the condense pipe.

I always have them function as a one-stop shop, even if shows a small cost. Just get plumber to provide the waste pipe close-by and sparky to provide a fused spur, and all other works are down to MVHR Co.

28

Window and Door Installation

The wiser ones amongst you will have decided to have one contractor supply and fix the windows and external doors. You will gone through the entire choosing and design process with both the architect and window supplier; bricky or timber frame manufacturer will have created the openings; and Window Co will have surveyed the as built opening sizes.

There are many British Standards (BS) and European Standards (ENs) that apply to both the manufacture and installation requirements of doors and windows, and then of course there are several building regulations to consider, which mainly hinge around safety glazing and any restricted or fire egress window openings;

Where windows and doors are to be replaced (but not where they are to be repaired only, as repair work does not fall within the definition of building work) the replacement work should comply with the requirements of Part L, Conservation of Fuel and Power, and Part N, Glazing – Protection Against Impact. In addition, after the work has been completed, the building should not have a lower level of compliance with the other applicable parts of Schedule 1. However, for all other applicable parts of building regulations, the windows or doors should either comply fully with the requirements of the approved documents or, if the item being replaced does not already fully comply, the replacement item should NOT make the noncompliance worse.

With new works, there are a few additional building regulations that come into play, namely Part B, Fire Safety; Part C, Resistance to Moisture; Part F, Ventilation; Part K, Protection from Falling; and Part M, Access and Use of Buildings.

Thermal Insulation

The windows will need to meet the applicable thermal insulation requirements of both the obvious regulations and the not-so-obvious building performance calculations: Take great care when ordering new windows to ensure that your supplier can prove the glazing units used will satisfy this requirement, as the BC surveyor could ask to see this proof before issuing a completion certificate. It would be a good idea that you leave any labels on the glazing in place until after a satisfactory inspection has been carried out by BC.

Safety Glazing

Low-level glazing (glazed areas within 800 mm of floor level) and glazing on doors within 1500 mm of floor level should generally be of a type so that if broken, they will break safely.

In practice, this means such glazing should be either laminated or toughened. Ordinary glazing can still be used in small pane sizes; however, this is only provided the glass is sufficiently strong to resist breakage. The approved document to Part N of the Building Regulations gives maximum sizes according to the thickness of glass – for example, in a single pane less than 1.1 m^2, 8 mm glass would be satisfactory.

Means of Escape

All first floor windows in dwellings should ideally have opening lights large enough to allow you to escape through them if you were trapped in the room by a fire. This also applies to rooms in bungalows that open into to a hall (unless the hall itself has an external door through which you could escape). To meet this requirement, all such windows should have an unobstructed openable area of at least 0.33 m^2 and be not less than 450 mm high and 450 mm wide (the route through the window may be at an angle rather than straight through). The bottom of the openable area should be less than 1100 mm above the floor.

It is not the a requirement of the Building Regulations to replace existing windows that do not have opening lights that meet the aforementioned requirements with windows that do, provided the replacement windows are no worse than those replaced in this respect. Where the existing windows already have opening lights that are larger than the preceding requirements, those in the new windows can be reduced in size, provided they are not reduced to less than the dimensions mentioned above.

Ventilation

Building Regulations require that adequate ventilation be provided for people in the building, and this should be considered when deciding on the size of opening lights in the replacement windows. For most rooms, one or more opening windows totalling 5% of the floor area, with background 'trickle' vents totalling 8,000 mm^2 will be adequate.

For kitchens, utility rooms, and bathrooms, an extract fan is also normally required. In some cases, the existing windows may contain a permanent vent to supply combustion air to a heating appliance, although this is now rare. If this is the case, however, you should ensure that either the replacement window contains a similar permanent vent, or that some other means of providing the required ventilation is installed at the same time.

Structural Safety

If the replacement windows are wider than those they replace, or if they involve the replacement of bay windows, then building control will need to be satisfied that a proper structural support has been provided above the window. In older buildings, the timber frame of the window was often sufficiently strong to carry the load of a wall or roof above it without a lintel. Obviously, in these cases, either a lintel needs to be installed when the window is replaced, or the new frame carefully reinforced to carry the load.

It is entirely possible that you will have a planning condition referring to 'Secure by Design', which speaks for itself and is included within the new Part Q Building Regulations in some areas. Very basically, these directives cover security issues such as the type of glazing and locking mechanisms used.

Then of course, you may have conservation restrictions on the window design. If you are doing works where the replacement of windows does not specifically fall under building regs' jurisdiction, you will need a Fenestration Self-Assessment Scheme (FENSA) certificate from the installers.

When replacing windows, doors, and roof lights in dwellings in England and Wales, homeowners must comply with current thermal performance and building regulation standards. FENSA enables companies that install replacement windows and doors to self-certify compliance under these building regulations without the need for a separate assessment from building control.

When it comes to installing windows, a serious consideration is one of airtightness. The window installer is also one of the key personnel on site who can make or break the airtightness strategy. Windows are one of the most common failure points when an airtightness test is been carried out on a building. While a window itself may, in theory, have an excellent level of airtightness, it is essential to ensure the installed window provides an airtight seal to the existing structure. If this is not attained, the integrity of the thermal performance of the window can be compromised. A passive window in particular can be the most expensive component within a low-energy building. There is little point in investing so much in a building component if it is not installed correctly.

One of the main reasons a window often proves to be one of the most common leakage points in a building is not just down to the complexity of the junction, but it is due to the ownership of responsibility on site in dealing with this detail. It is important from the outset to identify who is responsible for sealing the window to the building's airtightness layer when it is installed. Otherwise, the window installer and the internal membrane installer or plasterer will more than likely rely on each other to seal the junction, which in many cases, leads to no one sealing it in the end and the inevitable leak that ensues.

Applying airtightness tape before the window is installed is the preferable method of attaining airtightness on site. This is an expanding tape that is applied to the edge of the window in its compressed state. The window is then fitted into place and the tape is expanded by peeling away one side. This leaves an exposed edge of the tape, which can be linked to the internal membrane.

The timing of window fitting is always an issue: fit them too soon and they can (and will) be damaged when dropping the scaffold, or get covered in plaster; fit them too late and airtightness can be compromised.

There is no hard and fast rule to this conundrum, and the process is unique to each job. What I will say is that it is entirely possible that the windows are the most expensive single component in the entire build, so think VERY carefully.

29

Plastering Works

The title of this chapter should read plastering-associated works, since the chapter will include tacking (plaster-boarding) and insulation, plastering, floor screeding, and external rendering. Each is a trade all in its own, but the people involved blur between the numerous elements according to their abilities and wants.

A couple of nuances that all these trades have in common is that first, they work with the fast forward button pressed at all times, and second, they make a mess! With the first in mind, you need to be doubly sure that you are ready for them when they arrive – nothing worse than a frustrated plasterer who cannot get on with his job. On the second point, do not expect too much from them on the housekeeping front; they are artists, not menials who should be clearing up!

Like many other trades, you get plasterers (and associated trades) who are geared up for domestic works and others who are more at home with site work.

If the entire house is a new build, then the challenge is to find the right plasterers to suit the type of works. The exception to this is the tacker, who, due to the amount of work he needs to do in any one week, will cross over between the two types.

Now for some reason, an awful lot of plasterers hail from the Emerald Isle – must be something in the water (or Guinness). I will go as far as to say that most of the really good plasterers that I have encountered have been Irish, my mate Fergie being a case in point. If you have ever met me at a self-build exhibition, then chances are you will also have met Fergie. I take him as my foot soldier 'cos boy can he talk! And most of the time you can understand what he is saying! Unfortunately, this ability to talk means that 50% of what he says is anecdotal, 40% absolute rubbish, and the other 25% (? – he is Irish!) worth listening to. Since he focusses mainly on the plastering element, we will address the 25% in a minute.

In each case, plasterers are usually the only ones on site, so they do not really come into contact with other trades and just get about their business without too much drama.

From an H&S perspective, your main headache is scaffolding, both inside and outside, so they are relatively simple to provide for and police.

Although the Federation of Plastering and Drywall Contractors (FPDC) exists, the largest proportion of membership in the FPDC consists of specialist contractors. It is not really aimed at your average small firm or one-man band.

Before I go on to each aspect, one point I will discuss is that of price work versus daywork. Excluding mechanical trades (plumbing and electrical), most other tradesmen can lend themselves to either – it does not really work with plasterers.

There are numerous aspects that dictate the speed and therefore the effort they need to work, so most lads in these trades will work out how much work they can achieve in a day and then go home when that amount is finished. If you are paying them based on daywork – what appears to be a flagrant abuse of the daily rate – this could cause trouble.

Let me explain. Take your plasterer, who is putting material on the wall and ceiling as quickly as he can; then within a very specific timeframe, he has to trowel up the material to the required finish. Spread will work out exactly how much area he can achieve with the one 'hit' and then get cracking at blistering speed. Their usual discipline is two 'hits' a day with a break in between, which would rarely see them finishing work to coincide with the hours of a perceived daywork.

Make no mistake: this is a very physically demanding job. If your spread is worth his money, you will see him knackered by the end of his working day. By all means, agree a price with him based on how many days the job should take (let's face it – you will expect more than one wall per hit), and then let him get on with it. The same principle would apply to the other trades in this section. It is all backbreaking work, so you would rarely see a plastering associated tradesman on site later than say 3:00 pm.

Tacking (Plasterboarding)

I tend to lump any insulating or membrane-fixing works with the tacker's brief. The insulation, in whatever form, needs to go in just before the board is fixed, so it makes sense for him to fit it. If you are using a rigid PUR board that will double up as a vapour barrier, then make sure all the joints are sealed with tape.

Plasterboard nowadays is nearly always screwed on, with most tackers using collated screws and a special cordless screw gun. Collated screws are the drywall screws in a strip of plastic, which is fed into the gun like a machine gun, and works just about as quick! The screws will be fixed through the board at the rate of about one screw per second.

Even if you have decided to supply the board, let him supply the fixings as part of his price, as a part box of these screws left over is no good to you whatsoever. Also, when you are picking up the almost empty strips with a few screws left in it, your heart will be broken.

A few aspects to be borne in mind with the tacker:

Make sure you are using the correct thickness (density) board for the job. Most people think that the almost universal 12.5 mm thick board will do for all fixing to timber. The spacing of the timber joists or studs dictates this. You can span 400 mm centres without any lateral fixings (noggins) with 12.5 mm board. However, it is more cost effective when spanning 600 mm centres to use 15 mm board, or else you will be fitting perimeter noggins, which is more costly.

For this reason, most timber frame applications require 15 mm board. The above is actually covered in building regulations for the density of the board but often slips through the net. Not only that, you want the wall nice and stable when spread puts his skim coat on it.

A typical shortfall with tackers is to tack over cables or boxes that should have been brought out before fixing. This really winds up the sparky, and will you as well, when sparky has to dig holes in the wall or ceiling later. The only time that this works is when using downlighters that need a very specific sized hole to be cut in the board. If tacker has poked the cable through, then sparky will not be able to use his hole saw to cut a neat hole. It is best to have sparky make careful notes of the position, let tacker board over them and sparky fish them out later. Likewise, if sparky is using plasterboard clamping back boxes for the sockets and so on, it is easier to cut them later.

Although I have covered this elsewhere, make sure the plasterboard offcuts go into a dedicated skip for disposal.

If you are electing to drywall the plasterboard (dot and dab) to blockwork, (which in my opinion is an air-leakage nightmare), some tackers will do this for you; in other cases, the plasterer will do the job.

What I will say on this subject is that the eventual job is only as good as the number and position of the dabs of adhesive, and this job is difficult to police. There are very few applications where drylining is an advantage, and it is never on a new build, where we now have to consider air leakage and Accredited Construction methods.

Anyway, if you do feel the need to dryline, make sure there are plenty of adhesives around sparky's back boxes and the perimeter of the board, especially the top and bottom.

Plastering

Let us make no mistake – plastering is a skill that takes many years to perfect; not only the art of offering the plaster to the wall and making it stay there, but also a keen eye for straight and level. For these reasons, a good spread will not be cheap (be wary if he is!), and to a certain extent, he will be a taste arrogant.

If plastering on to brick or block, then spread will be applying the 'float and set' method. The idea is that he lays a thick (float) coat of either sand and cement or gypsum hardwall to bring the wall flat. With most new builds nowadays, gypsum plaster is the preferred method, since it does not crack later. Following that, usually the next day with gypsum, he will then 'set' the work with a thin coat of much smoother plaster, which is mixed to the consistency of custard.

If plastering over plasterboard, spread will scrim (like a strip of bandage) over the joints, then apply the skim coat in the same way as above.

A couple of things to watch out for here, which mainly applies to lads more used to working on site with a mass production mentality:

The skim coat should be put on in two thin passes, one immediately after the other. The first is to level out the imperfections, and the second is what is trowelled up to the mirror-like surface, but also to assist with the setting (drying out) procedure. There are a lot of spreads out there who will simply concentrate on getting 'pink' on the wall as much and as quick as possible and only apply one pass because it is quicker. Quite simply, you are being shortchanged, and you will end up with dimples or crazing, which will not show up for a few days.

Another thing to police is the accuracy of the angle beads on corners. They need to be level and upright especially on window reveals.

Speaking of window reveals, make sure that cavity closures are installed before the windows. Apart from forming an insulated vertical DPC across the cavity, the closures stop the possibility of moisture transmission from the external brickwork into the plaster (or plasterboard) on the reveal. I always specify that before either plasterboarding or wet plastering the reveals, a line of silicone should be applied between the cavity closure and the window frame as a belt and braces job.

A good spread will clean out sparky's back boxes as he goes along. If he does not, knocking the hard plaster out later will take with it a fair amount more than it should, leaving you with making good at decorating stage around sparky's faceplates.

I have known spreads who completely cover sparky's box and cables, which is missed all through the job and only manifests when sparky tries to test at the end, or when you wonder where the socket is that you asked for beside the bed.

This particular trade is without doubt the potentially messiest trade of the entire works. If you think about it, spread is handling a material that at best wants to slide off his trowel or wall. At worst, he is trying to lay material with the viscosity of yoghurt above his head.

He will make a mess, and to be fair, sometimes it is easier to let the plaster 'go off' before trying to clean it up rather than spread it about, except where it has dripped down the new window frame. This needs washing off whilst wet or it will possibly scratch the window if you try to remove it after it has hardened.

I purposely have not refereed to lime plastering, mainly to be found in renovation or listed works. This is a very specialist subject that requires expert application, and definitely should be left to dedicated contractors. Many of the general aspects apply, but this work – mainly because the requirements and principles go beyond the actual plastering itself – would deserve a chapter or even a small book in its own right.

Floor Screed

There are fundamentally two types of floor screeding, that in turn have two completely different ways of laying: sand and cement screed and anhydrite (calcium sulphite) screed. The two options are almost considered different trades in their own right, and laying them requires a different set of skills. I am sure that the more traditional floor layers (sand and cement) will argue that much less skill is required to lay liquid screed.

Except for buildings where the concrete slab is left exposed, such as a warehouse, all concrete floors are covered with a screed layer, which provides a final level finish onto the floor covering that has been installed: tiles, carpet, wood, and so on.

When underfloor heating is installed, perimeter wall insulation and floor insulation panels with a fitted moisture barrier are installed on the floor slab, and the underfloor pipework is secured to the panels. This is then covered with the final screed layer.

The screed has to be of suitable depth for strength and to provide sufficient cover over the underfloor heating pipework to prevent it from cracking. When installed over floor insulation, the screed is called a floating screed.

Sand and cement screed (with added fibres)
Sand and cement screeds are a mixture of sand and cement generally in a 4:1 mixture ratio with water. Fibres can be added, which reduce surface abrasion and micro-cracking on the screed surface.

Sand and cement enhanced screed
Enhanced screeds are sand and cement screeds with added chemicals that improve the properties of the standard screed. The improved properties include faster drying times and/or extra strength. Pre-mix screeds usually fall into this category.

Anhydrite (calcium sulphite) screed
Anhydrite screeds are a type of screed different from sand and cement. The screed is made from calcium sulphate, sand,

water, and other chemicals to form a liquid screed. Unlike sand and cement screeds (which are spread, compacted, and levelled), the screed is poured on the floor through a delivery hose and levelled with a dappling bar. Large areas can be covered much quicker with this screed type. It is essential, however, that the floor and edge insulation must be fully waterproofed by taping and sealing all joints in this insulation. These screeds are delivered to site ready mixed.

Whilst a large area of this screed can be installed quickly, it has a disadvantage that does not allow it to be laid in wet areas or laid to falls, and requires a decent area to make it cost effective.

Liquid cementitious screed
This type of screed is similar to an anhydrite screed but uses cement instead of calcium sulphate. It is generally much stronger and can be a rapid-drying screed, which, although available, is not as commonly used.

Liquid screeds are considered a more efficient alternative for wet underfoot heating since the screed is water based and completely envelopes the pipe, therefore allowing better heat transfer into the floor itself.

Expansion joints-crack inducers
All screeds expand and contract to some degree, so allowance has to be made for this. The perimeter insulation fitted with underfloor heating allows for some of this expansion or contraction. However, large areas will need to have expansion joints or crack inducer cuts in the screed itself to allow movement and avoid screed cracking. Expansion joints will also be required to mirror any expansion joints in the floor slab. These should be as recommended by the screeder or architect, and the need for these is often underestimated.

Where the screed is to be finished with a rigid tile, marble, or stone, topping the expansion provisions is critical, as screed movement can crack the floor finish. The flooring should be designed by the floor installer detailing the provision for expansion in the floor tiles themselves. This can then be mirrored with a separate bedding layer with expansion joints, or in the screed below.

Day joints
Day joints are positions where the screed has been finished on one day and will be carried on the next day. In these positions, to avoid cracking, the joint needs to be reinforced with mesh to bond the screed together. Alternatively, an expansion joint could be fitted in this position.

Reinforcing mesh
In the sand and cement type screeds, the use of D49 mesh or chicken wire, or an SBR slurry consisting of polymer, cement, and water can be used to reinforce the screed to avoid cracking. In areas where a number of underfloor circuits can come together, such as some manifold locations, or where the screed is below the recommended thickness, the screed should be reinforced by the installation of D49 mesh, at midpoint in the screed, over the underfloor pipework.

Rendering

Rendering in layman terms is the equivalent of external plastering. Traditionally, rendering was used to cover poor-quality external walls, but in more modern times, has become a decorative feature.

There are mainly two types of render: sand and cement–based and acrylic, often referred to as monocouche (French for one coat) systems.

Both require skills similar to that of the plasterer, but that does not necessarily mean that the same spread plastering inside will want to work on an external surface and vice versa.

Sand and cement render:

This render is a mortar, consisting basically of cement and fine aggregate, usually together with lime or a plasticizer, which is applied to a wall surface, generally in two or more coats. When correctly matched with the background, the hardened render provides a durable weather-resistant finish.

An ideal rendering mortar should generally be slightly weaker than the background to which it will be applied. This also applies to the coats in a multi-coat rendering system – each successive coat should be no stronger than the previous coat. In practice, this is frequently achieved by maintaining constant mix proportions but using successively thinner coats. Whilst there are some specially formulated rendering mortars available that can be applied in a single coat, they are not generally used in a professional way.

The properties of the background should be considered. In other words, a cement-based render should not be applied over an on old lime mortar wall, as it will be much stronger and will therefore cause problems with the wall breathing, subsequently resulting in cracking.

The degree of suction can also be a significant factor in achieving proper adhesion. It may be necessary to adjust this by pre-treatment or the use of admixtures.

Sand and cement rendering is normally more subjected to environmental exposure (for example, frost, wind, sun and rain). It will also require, in most cases, a paint or the like coating to finalise the protection. Therefore, the location of the structure to which the rendering will be applied will also affect the ability of the rendering to withstand the environmental actions applied to it.

For all of the above reasons, many new build warranty providers will no longer accept the use of sand and cement render systems.

Lime render:
Green self-builders love lime, and it has some advantages over cement renders, in that it is inherently more flexible than cement and you are less likely to have problems with moisture being trapped within the wall – a problem when cement renders are applied to old walls.

Lime also tends to look very appealing, though it does require frequent coats of lime wash. Building limes are available in a variety of forms, from traditional lime putties (which are bought wet by the tub) through to a number of bagged products – hydraulic limes – which behave rather like a weak cement. They need to be mixed on site with good quality sand, and are hand-trowelled in the traditional way. Limes are a little more expensive than standard cement renders, and they take a little take longer to apply.

Synthetic renders:
One of the major attractions of this type of render is that they come in colours and thus do not need painting (or re-painting in a few years). In contrast to sand and cement, a monocouche render is supplied in bag form ready for mixing with water: it can be applied by hand trowel or sprayed on.

These type of renders are split into two types. The first is where a cement-based base coat is applied, following which a top acrylic or silicone-based 'thin coat' is applied. The second, which is a true monocouche, is coloured and applied in one thick coat.

We then have polymer renders, the most modern products in the market, which contain white Portland cement. Polymer renders incorporate silicone water repellents as an integral part of the lime render application of the cement based render system. This silicon technology imparts a high degree of water repellence to the render surface whilst allowing water vapour to pass through the render, thus allowing the substrate to breathe. The use of nylon-reinforced base coats provides a high-strength base for the finish coat. Polymer render is available as monocouche render, eliminating the need for a base coat. Monocouche renders are usually only applied to new lightweight blocks or medium-dense concrete blocks. Expansion joints often need to be used to ensure that the render does not crack.

Colour-matched PVC corner beads and stop beads can be used to enhance appearance. Each have advantages according to the surface you are rendering on to – blockwork or external render – and therefore need to be carefully specified. I would always recommend that they be applied by a manufacturer-approved installer.

With either of these renders, you would be expecting a complete system guarantee.

One last thing I will mention is that if you are choosing a rendered surface on a new build timber frame, be wary of using the batten-and-carrier board system fixed to the timber frame, as opposed to a block outer skin. Both are good alternatives in their own right, but many mortgage companies do not like the former systems, so any prospective buyer of the property may have issues. In reality, when all sums are added up, there is not much in it cost-wise, so I would always lean towards block outer skin.

Vince Holden

30

Decorating

Painters and decorators use a range of coverings to enhance and protect surfaces. These surfaces could include plaster, metal, and wood.

A decent decorator should have good practical and creative skills. He or she must be able to work carefully and pay attention to detail, and need a good head for heights.

Now it is an unfortunate reality that if there is one trade in the industry that Mr and Mrs will elect to do themselves to save money, it's the decorating. It is also an unfortunate reality that in such a case, very rarely is the job completed well, if at all!

There is an old saying in the industry: 'If you can p*** you can paint.' And to an extent, we have all, at some time, painted our own bedroom.

However, the above is just construction banter; decorating is a trade to be learned with its own skills – good and not so good – as with any other trade.

What I have never fathomed out is why someone would want to spend all sorts of money on the build but not consider the part that makes it all look pretty and complete, worthy of a professional. The decorating stage of a job is the best bit: it shows off the works and brings the entire concept together with lovely clean lines and fresh surfaces – if done well!

You would be better off hanging the doors and fixing the skirtings and architraves yourself and getting a professional decorator to, shall we say, 'enhance' the works, than the other way round.

Decorators always have pimped up vans and possess a radio more at home in a high-class recording studio. They will have pet names for all of their brushes (reach towards one of them and you will lose your hand) that will be kept in neat order in a specially designed bombproof cabinet. Ask to borrow one of their Siberian sable masterpieces and you will be treated to a look of incredulity usually reserved for if you had asked to marry their 14-year-old daughter. They will know the different scientific formulas of emulsion and eggshell, and don't even get them started on using 'them posh paints' against Dulux Trade.

An experienced, decent decorator will live his life to disciplines and indulge in hobbies such as bookbinding or taxidermy, which will reflect in how he approaches his work – carefully and methodically.

Decorators live in a very insular world on site. When they arrive to share their artistry, everyone else should be gone, the entire works be operating theatre clean, and of course, the ambient temperature at 18.75 degrees.

Decorators always wear shorts under their whites, even in January!

Oh and one last attribute – they are never wrong ... Ever!

Formally trained decorators are quite a rarity these days with City & Guilds and NVQ providing several levels of skill training, but to be fair, once a decent level of fundamental knowledge is achieved, then it's down to experience that proves how good a decorator is. Quite simply, the best way to gauge the prowess of decorator is to see some of his work and talk to his customers. There really is no substitute for word of mouth in this trade.

Be suspicious of a decorator who could start work on Monday. You would usually have to book a good decorator immediately after receiving your planning approval, if not sooner. He also does not like filling his pimped up ride with diesel too often, as he only works locally. Think of it like you buying the house/plot so your daughter is in the catchment area of a particular prep school. Find the decorator first, then go looking for your building plot.

As far as accredited bodies are concerned, we have the Painting & Decorating Association (PDA), which is the UK's largest trade association for the painting and decorating industry. The PDA promotes professionalism and integrity, and represents thousands of contractors in the field of painting and decorating. The main focus of the PDA is to ensure that all members of the association adhere to the highest quality standards. The London Association of Master Decorators (LAMD) is also united with the PDA. Members of the PDA are required to be qualified, fully insured, follow a code of conduct, provide high quality work to customers, and be familiar with the latest technologies in the industry.

The British Decorators Association (formerly known as the National Federation of Master Painters and Decorators of England and Wales) is a national organisation, which caters to the needs of professionals in the painting and decorating industry within the UK. The aim of the British Decorators' Association is to promote and enhance the status and business standards of its members in the industry. In order to become a member of this association, the applicant must be fully insured; qualified; able to produce quality work; up-to-date with the latest painting and decorating technologies; and follow a code of conduct as set by the British Decorators' Association.

However, in my opinion, decorating – as far as capability credentials are concerned – does not require membership to an organisation in the same way as say a heating engineer does. He is either good at the right money, or he is not, and you can usually tell very easily.

On the H&S front, the issues mainly hinge around working at heights and Control of Substances Hazardous to Health (COSHH). The first issue speaks for itself, but the second regarding substances should not be taken lightly. Several materials within the decorators' jurisdiction can cause skin and respiratory problems, not least of all, lead in some older paints.

On to the works themselves:

Assuming you have seen the light and decided to employ professionals, there is no point at all in getting decorator in too soon. It is tempting to have them start whilst other works are going on, but this is not at all productive. The only time that this method is relaxed is if decorator wants to come in and mist coat all the walls and ceilings before second fix works by other trades proceed.

One decorator that I have worked with for a dozen years wants to come in once the plaster is dry and spray coat all the walls and ceilings. It costs a taste more but gives him a good head start later on.

Decorator will want to work on as many completed areas as possible so he can go right through the entire works: first, preparing; then, first coating and second coating on the entire job if possible. He first wants to make all the dust created while rubbing down hoovered up before he even gets one of his pride and joy brushes or rollers out, so you will want to get this done to all of the works and not just a couple of rooms at a time. You will be surprised at how quickly he can put a coat of paint on a room.

On the subject of preparation, before getting the brushes out, beware the decorator who has been using the same piece of glass paper all week and starts to paint within an hour of arriving. Preparation is everything for a good decorator – by the time he opens a tin of paint, all the hard work should be done, and he will be on the home straight.

His biggest enemy is dirt and dust, whether created by himself or others, so a major piece of his kit will be a decent industrial hoover, as the last thing he wants is dust in the paint.

When decorators are on site, they own it, and for a good reason. It's their job to turn your soon to be home, from a building site into a finished work of art, and the last thing they want is for the groundworker to be sitting inside in muddy boots, eating his pot noodle and leaving wet tea bags all over the place when decorator is working his magic. Decorators are not part of the hardhat and steel toecap brigade for a reason, and they are the only ones forgiven for working in soft trainers – but no flip-flops!

It never ceases to amaze me when I see the brickies battered old mixer parked in the middle of the kitchen when decorator is trying to make the place look pretty. The mixer is probably worth about £4, but bricky is convinced that the only place for it is chained to the £30k hand-built kitchen cabinets, or there will be a queue of scoundrels opening their transit doors the minute his back is turned. By this stage of the job, the only items that should be inside the house should either be fixed to the wall or holding a paintbrush!

One last point that I touched on earlier: don't be tempted to use cheap paint. First, you will use twice as much of it, and second, because of this, you will use more labour to apply it, so it will cost you more. Ironically, the same can apply to some very expensive paints as well!

It is not widely known, but a main brand paint sold in DIY stores is not the same quality (thickness and cover capabilities) as that sold under the trade guise by paint merchants; that is why it's cheaper!

31

Finishings

I have decided not to write a chapter on Finishing's.

Finishing items could include;
- Wall coverings - tile or wallpaper even.
- Floor coverings - tile, wood, carpet, polished concrete.
- Kitchen cabinets etc.
- Bathroom fittings.
- Final joinery

In other words; the pretty bits at the end.

The list is never ending and the permutations infinite, as there are zillions of magazines, books and people out there to advise. Therefore, you do not need me offering my two-penneth and stereotyping the people involved (as if!)

I am not an interior designer - not good looking enough and prefer to wear clothes that fit me, so best we leave this subject.

32

External Works

Just a short chapter on the last bit.

Generally speaking, external work at the end of the job is an extension of the groundwork conducted at the beginning of the job. With this in mind, it is useful to have an idea at the beginning as to what the end product external works will involve, so things like any surface water drainage/soakaways and ducting can be incorporated in Groundwork Co's original scope of work. If you are fortunate enough to know exactly what external works will be required, much of the basic hardscaping can form part of Groundwork Co's quote, but segregated from the earlier works. If this is the case, Groundwork Co will quite possibly carry out some of the hardscaping fundaments at early doors to make his life easier at the end. The quote should hopefully reflect this. For example, he may choose to base out the drive with hardcore as part of the early works whilst the larger machine (digger) is on site, meaning he only needs to bring in a smaller machine at the end.

Conversely, there's no point in throwing all the refurb brick rubble in a pile to the rear during the works because it's easy, only to find later that the pile is six times higher than the modest patio you are building, and the newly built extension means you have to lug 20 tonnes around to skips at the front of the house in wheelbarrows. I'd love a £10 note for every time I have seen that!

Planning conditions could heavily dictate what hard and softscaping you need to include. Typical issues could be porous surfaces on hardstanding or parking areas, actual positions of planting areas, and the type of plants to be included. If this is the case, you will have submitted a landscape proposal that will indicate what goes where to satisfy the planning condition. Planners are concerned with the right plants and trees for the area and the position they will sit in, in order to obtain the right amount of sunlight and so on. Also on the plan will be such items as parking areas and boundary treatments (fencing and so on).

So what is the difference between hardscape and softscape?

In the context of landscape management, hardscape and softscape are both elements in landscaping, which essentially refer to the heavy or light landscape materials used respectively. While the stone, concrete, tarmac, and brick elements are referred to as hardscape, trees, soil, flowerbeds, vegetable gardens, grass and shrubs constitute the softscape. Hardscape takes care of the spaces, proportion, patios, driveways, and gates. Softscape recognises plants, flowers, colour scheme, and pattern of planting.

A combination of hardscape design and softscape decision effectively forms the landscaping, and therefore the external works.

Hardscaping is usually completed first with heavy materials and machines to match. The softscape follows on and usually completed by hand or smaller machines.

So, earlier when planning the site and any preparatory groundwork, if you need to provide permeable parking or a driveway, Groundwork Co would need to know this because the hardcore (Type 3) would have to be the correct one to enable water to permeate through. There's no point in laying truckloads of the wrong hardcore that will not do the job later, thus having to dig it all out again.

Just briefly, the difference between the widely recognised Ministry of Transport (MOT) aggregates – commonly types 1, 2, and 3 – is the amount of 'finings' (small particles and dust) found in the mix.

Type 1 has a large amount of finings, thus enabling the surface to be compacted, knitted together, and rolled almost smooth. Type 3 has virtually no finings, therefore making it ideal for a permeable surface to allow the water to drain through. Obviously, Type 2 is somewhere in between. Both recycled crushed concrete and the crushed rock 'scalpings' can be categorised accordingly but without getting too complicated, whilst not all conform to MOT standards, unless you are building a highways-inspected motorway through your back garden, its only generally necessary to focus on the level of finings according to the need for permeability.

In most cases, the aggregates would form the sub-base with, say, block paving, permeable tarmac, or stone chippings dressing the surface and making it look pretty.

Since we nowadays focus more on sustainable drainage systems (SUDs), any permeable areas could be an integral part of the overall design, especially if your plot slopes or you are on difficult soil. Do not underestimate the need for decent ground drainage, which is relatively easy to incorporate if timed right.

No need for me to waffle on about the many ways to dress your externals; there are many books out there dedicated to the subject. However, when it comes to planting, especially if building according to the landscape design you had to create to satisfy a planning condition, what I will say is plan the timing according to the plants/shrubs decided, or vice versa.

There are lots of shrubs (because that's what planners are mainly concerned with) that can only be bought and planted at certain times of the year, so give this some thought when designing, which of course could have been many months earlier.

This is the stage of the job where we are making everything look pretty and complete, so the jobs need an artistic flair – something you will either have or not. If not, my advice is to get some help. I know a garden evolves over time, but the fundaments need to be planned. It's not easy to keep moving your patio or trees when you discover that the sun actually rises in the east and sets in the west, not the other way around!

33

And Finally

Hopefully, by reading this book, you will have an insight into the fickle world of construction, and now know what to expect.

All being well, you will have reached the end of the project without too many hiccups, and the ones you did encounter, you were able to deal with skilfully.

Not that hard was it?

Maestro

The maestro lowered his arms, let out a long breath, and smiled at his orchestra. He was very pleased with the performance. All of the lessons learned from the virtuoso in his book had proved invaluable; he knew that he could not have navigated his first time without it.

There had been a couple of hiccups; on a few occasions, one or two musicians had lost their timing and the maestro had had to bring them back to avoid upsetting the entire performance. Another time, later on in the concert, the maestro himself had felt overwhelmed; he was trying too hard, which resulted in him losing his patience. So the more experienced section leaders of his team had carried on, temporarily guiding the maestro and indeed the entire performance until he gathered his thoughts. They were after all professionals, and this was his first major presentation. He had chosen well, and he knew that all the hard work at the planning stage had paid off.

Maestro took a few moments to look back over the performance, remembering where he could improve and also where he should feel very proud. To take on such a large task with limited experience had taken all of his resolve and nerve. It could after all have gone horribly wrong.

He stepped away from the lectern and embraced his followers. The feelings of personal reward from this successful achievement were already proving addictive, with him wondering when he should begin looking towards the next project ...

Sign up for my newsletter at www.vinceholden.com to receive regular updates on other valuable articles and notifications.

* To contact me for free advice, send me an email at the following address:

advice@vinceholden.co.uk

* * * *

I would not be able to consider this work of art complete without mentioning my wife Michelle;
Writing such a book(s) is a laborious task and with this being my second volume, the novelty of me spending social hours, including holidays, tapping away on my iPad, or ensconced in my office, wore off for the 1ˢᵗ Lady quite a while ago.

Whilst my passion for both my work and the industry is fully understood in the Holden household, her patience has been seriously tested.

Thank you for your tolerance my love. I.L.U.T.O.S.A.B.A.Z.X.

* * * *

ABOUT THE AUTHOR

Vince Holden has 45 years' experience in construction. He began his career from school with a local construction company that specialised in timber frame construction, obtaining an apprenticeship in carpentry and joinery, and then carrying on with education in site management and surveying. By the time he formed Holden Management Services to focus on Project Management in 2010, Vince's all-embracing experience had taken him through sub-contract carpentry, his own roofing company, and then on to wide-ranging construction and house building. His strong work ethos enabled him to maintain the exemplary status of A1 Zurich Warranty Registered Builder for 15 years.

Vince is passionate about and has many years of experience in the sustainability sector, working on renewable technology, energy efficiency, and related matters. He has worked on developing and proving new technologies, reducing energy costs and the environmental impact of buildings. His extensive knowledge of traditional masonry and system build such as timber frame construction, places him in a position to offer advice on the management of numerous methods of domestic build.

In 2012, Vince Holden was accepted into the Chartered Institute of Building.

Vince is married to Michelle, and blessed with a daughter and two sons. He lives with his wife, their two dogs, a parrot, and, at the time of writing, three ducks and nine chickens, in an old farmhouse in north Hampshire.

Glossary

Since, inherently, we tend to use abbreviations and acronyms, I thought it best to give a brief explanation of each one.

ACD - Accredited Construction Details - performance standards required to demonstrate compliance with the energy efficiency requirements (Part L) of the Building Regulations.

ACM - Asbestos Containing Materials

ARB - Architects Registration Board

ASHP - Air Source Heat Pump - is a system which transfers heat from outside to inside a building, or vice versa, under the principles of vapour compression refrigeration.

BoQ - Bill of Quantities - is a document used in tendering whre materials, parts, and labour are quantified, itemized and costed.

BR - Building Regulations.

BRE - Building Research Establishment is a former UK government establishment (but now a private organisation) that carries out research, consultancy and testing for the construction sectors in the United Kingdom.

BREEAM (BREDEM) - Building Research Establishment Environmental Assessment Methodology - sets the standard for best practice in sustainable building design, construction and operation and has become one of the most comprehensive and widely recognised measures of a building's environmental performance.

CAD (Autocad) - AutoCAD is a computer-aided drafting software program used for creating blueprints for buildings. Usually creates files in dwg format

CDM - Construction Design & Management (Health & Safety) - See chapter

CIAT - Chartered Institute of Architectural Technologists - is the lead qualifying body for Architectural Technology and represents those practising and studying within the discipline.

CIOB - Chartered Institute of Building - is the world's largest and most influential professional body for construction management and leadership.

CISE - Chartered Institution of Structural Engineers - is the world's leading professional body for qualifications and standards in structural engineering.

CLS - Canadian Lumber Standard - was originally manfactured in Canada for use in the building of **timber** framed houses, hence it's name.
Over the past few years **CLS** has become increasingly popular in the UK for use as framing for stud walls and internal partitions.

CPP - Construction Phase Plan

CSH - Code for Sustainable Homes - is the national standard for the sustainable design and construction of new homes.

CSCS - Construction Skills Certification Scheme - Proof that an operative has at least fundamental health and safety knowledge

CFC's - chlorofluorocarbon
HFC's - hydrofluorocarbons
HCFC's - hydro chlorofluorocarbons - gasses associated with the "Greenhouse effect" and harm to the ozone layer

DER/ TER - The Dwelling Emission Rate (*DER*) and the Target Emission Rate (*TER*) are the headline Co2 figures which SAP Calculations measure.

DOE - Department Of the Environment (also EA - Environment Agency)

DPC - Damp Proof Course

DPM – Damp Proof Membrane

EPDM - ethylene propylene diene monomer (M-class) rubber Used a s a flat roof membrane

ECD - Enhanced Construction Details – next generation of ACD's (see above)

EL Insurance – Employers Liability Insurance

EPS – Expanded Polystyrene
XPS – Extruded Polystyrene

EPC – Energy Performance Certificate - gives a property an energy efficiency rating from A (most efficient) to G (least efficient) and is valid for 10 years.

EU – European Union

F10 – Notification form to HSE

FDN – FounDatioN - concrete mix

FRA - Flood Risk Assessment

FSC - Forest Stewardship Council - certificate verifies forest products along the production chain of processing and transformation, and ensures that the timber is sourced from a sustainable location.

GSHP - Ground Source Heat Pump

GPS – Global Positioning System

HMRC – Her Majesty's Revenue and Customs

HSE – Health and Safety Executive

HVAC - Heating Ventilating Air Conditioning

ICF – Insulated Concrete Formwork

IDDA - Interior Decorators and Designers Association.

JCT - Joint Contracts Tribunal - produces standard forms of **contract** for construction, guidance notes and other standard documentation for use in the construction industry.

LABC – Local Authority Building Control - represent building control teams in councils across England, but also confusingly is the name of LABC Warranty, a private company who work in partnership with Local Authority

LPA - Local Planning Authority

LPG - Liquified Petroleum Gas - also referred to as simply propane or butane.

MDPE – Medium-Density Polythene – usually used for underground water or gas pipe

MMC – Modern Methods of Construction

MPAN - Meter Point Administration Number, also know as Supply Number or S-Number, is a 21-digit reference used to uniquely identify electricity supply points such as individual domestic residences.

MPRN - Meter Point Reference Number – gas equivalent of the above.

Mr & Mrs SB – Mr & Mrs Self-Builder

MVHR – Mechanical Ventilation Heat recovery - see chapter

NPPF - National Planning Policy Framework

NHBC – National House Builders Council – Usually associated with Structural Warranty insurance

OSB - Oriented Strand Board also known as sterling board, sterling board, is an engineered wood particle **board** formed by adding adhesives and then compressing layers of wood strands (flakes) in specific orientations.

Pa – Pascals – measurement of air pressure

P&O – Profits and Overheads

PC sum – Prime Cost Sum - is the cost of an item that has either not been selected or the price was unknown at the time the contact was entered into, but will be eventually nominated by the client

PCI - Pre Construction Information (CDM)

Prov Sum - Provisional sum - is an allowance, usually estimated, that is inserted into tender documents for a specific element of the works that is not yet defined in enough detail for tenderers to price. This, together with a brief description, allows tenderers to apply mark up and attendance costs within their overall tender price.

PD – Permitted Development

PI insurance - Professional Indemnity Insurance - is provided by a professional to cover compensation he or she may need to pay to correct a mistake or cover any legal costs due to negligence, such as giving incorrect advice or making a mistake in your work.
PL insurance - Public Liability Insurance
EL Insurance - Employers Libility Insurance

PM - Project Manager

PUR/PIR - Rigid polyurethane (PUR) and polyisocyanurate (PIR) insulation - products are highly effective, lightweight and many have the ability to bond to most materials. Found commonly in Rigid insulation boards and SIP panels, but also now as adhesives(PU glue)

QS - Quantity Surveyor - Creates amongst other things the BoQ (above)

RIBA - Royal Institute of British Architects - is a professional body for architects (see chapter).

RICS - Royal Institute of Chartered Surveyors - is a professional body that accredits professionals within the land, property and construction sectors.

Robust Details - is a set of details created in response to the housebuilding industry's request for an alternative to pre-completion sound testing as a means of satisfying the sound insulation requirements of the building regulations (in England and Wales).

SAP - Standard Assessment Procedure - is the calculation that is required in order to produce a Predicted Energy Assessment and a Energy Performance Certificate.

Section 106 - The council can enter into a Section 106 agreement, otherwise known as a 'planning obligation', with a developer where it is necessary to provide contributions to offset negative impacts caused by construction and development.

Section 80,81 - Demolition Notice - notification given to the Local Authority that demolition works are to take place.

SIP - Structutal Insulated Panael - Timber frame

SoW - Schedule of Works - (see chapter)

S&F - Supply and Fix

SMM - Standard Method of Measurement - provides detailed information, classification tables and rules for measuring building works. SMM7 is typically used in the preparation of bills of quantities, and specifications in tender documentation, providing a uniform basis for measuring building works in order to facilitate industry wide consistency.

SUDS - Sustainable Drainage System

TBC - To Be Confirmed
TF - Timber Frame

TFEE - Target Fabric Energy Efficiency - part of the SAP calculation

U Value - see chapter

UKTFA - UK Timber Frame Association

VAT - Value Added Tax

VCL - Vapour Control Layer
VCM - Vapour Control Membrane

VOC - Volatile Organic Compound

Printed in Great Britain
by Amazon